God Knows
His Name

God Knows His Name

The True
Story of
John Doe
No. 24

Dave Bakke

With a Foreword by
Mary Chapin Carpenter

Southern Illinois University Press
Carbondale and Edwardsville

Copyright © 2000 by the Board of Trustees,
Southern Illinois University
Foreword © 2000 by Mary Chapin Carpenter
All rights reserved
Printed in the United States of America
03 02 01 00   4 3 2 1

Library of Congress Cataloging-in-Publication Data

Bakke, David, 1951–
    God knows his name : the true story of John Doe no. 24 / Dave Bakke ;
with a foreword by Mary Chapin Carpenter.
        p. cm.
    1. Doe, John, d. 1993. 2. Deaf—Illinois—Biography. 3. Inmates of
institutions—Illinois—Biography. 4. Depersonalization—Illinois—Case
studies. I. Title.

    HV2534.D63 B35 2000
    362.4'2'092—dc21
    [B]
    ISBN 0-8093-2326-5 (cloth : alk. paper)
    ISBN 0-8093-2327-3 (pbk. : alk. paper)   00-020070

The paper used in this publication meets the minimum requirements of
American National Standard for Information Sciences—Permanence of Paper
for Printed Library Materials, ANSI Z39.48-1992. ⊗

9/07

What we see, over and over again, is that there's a resiliency of the human spirit that is not going to be destroyed. It's not going to just survive, it's going to win. John is a good example of that.

—Sister Bernadette Wynne,
Helen Keller National Center for
Deaf-Blind Youths and Adults,
Sands Point, New York

Contents

Illustrations

Foreword

A few years ago, I wrote a song called "John Doe No. 24." I was inspired by the obituary of a person of the same name that I happened to read one day in the *New York Times*. I was captivated by this account of a life and deeply moved by it as well. Although the article was quite brief, it managed to convey the isolation he experienced throughout his life and suggested how profoundly his lack of identity affected those who became his caretakers. As I began writing, I tried to imagine his thoughts, his feelings, and the journeys his heart may have taken throughout his life, as he was confined to one institution after another. The song took final shape when I found the music to blend the words with. It was a circular melody, one that seemed to me to complement the imagined story.

It never crossed my mind that someday I might write a foreword to a book about John Doe No. 24's life when I finished the song. Clearly, he inspired more than a few people during his life and after it was over.

Mary Chapin Carpenter

John Doe No. 24

I was standing on this sidewalk in 1945 in Jacksonville, Illinois
When asked what my name was there came no reply
They said I was a deaf and sightless half-wit boy
But Lewis was my name though I could not say it
I was born and raised in New Orleans
My spirit was wild so I let the river take it
On a barge and a prayer upstream

They searched for a mother and they searched for a father
And they searched til they searched no more
The doctors put to rest their scientific tests
And they named me John Doe No. 24
And they all shook their heads in pity
For a world so silent and dark
Well there's no doubt that life's a mystery
But so too is the human heart

And it was my heart's own perfume when the crape jasmine bloomed
    on St. Charles Avenue
Though I couldn't hear the bells of the streetcars coming
By toeing the track I knew
And if I were an old man returning
With my satchel and pork pie hat
I'd hit every jazz joint on Bourbon
And I'd hit every one on Basin after that

The years kept passing as they passed me around
From one state ward to another
Like I was an orphaned shoe from the lost and found
Always missing the other
They gave me a harp last Christmas
And all the nurses took a dance
Lately I've been growing listless
Been dreaming again of the past

I'm wandering down to the banks of the Great Big Muddy
Where the shotgun houses stand
I am seven years old and I feel my daddy
Reach out for my hand
While I drew breath no one missed me
So they won't on the day that I cease
Put a sprig of crape jasmine with me
To remind me of New Orleans

I was standing on this sidewalk in 1945 in Jacksonville, Illinois

Acknowledgments

The author wishes to thank the following people, without whose assistance John's life would have remained lost:

Lincoln: Larry Bussard, Adolph Phillips, Arlie Joyner, Bob Gephart, Carolyn George, Albert, Richard Cutts, Jerry Cisco, Dale Awick, Steve Sievers, Ann Klose.

Jacksonville: Mary Ransdell, Willie Glaze, Harriet Connor, Shirlee Pettit, Don Cook, John Goebel, Kitty Aubry.

Springfield: Ann Patla, Mary Haas Doehring, Jo Warfield, Judith Hollenberg, Dr. Lynn Pardie, Mark Pence, Terry and Janet Borkgren, Carlissa Puckett, Dr. Jonathan Hess, SPARC.

New York: Joseph McNulty, Barbara Hausman, Sister Bernadette Wynne, Peter Krienbihl, Sue Ruzenski, Brian McCarroll.

Peoria: Eric Sutter, Barbara Smiley, Angie Bergquist, Kim Cornwell, Donna Romine, Kevin Pilger, Judy Lutz.

Introduction

At the Sharon Oaks Nursing Home in Peoria, Illinois, nurse Donna Romine stood next to the bed of a dying resident. It was 28 November 1993. In the bed was a graying black man who had no sight, no hearing, and no speech. He also had no name other than the one the state had given him: John Doe No. 24.

Romine knew it would be just a matter of moments before John Doe No. 24 would be gone. In those last few seconds, she reflected sadly on the mystery of a man no one knew. Somewhere, she thought, he had a family. There were people who cared about him and wondered where he had been in the fifty years since he had disappeared. There were people somewhere who knew his real name. Now, with his death, he took with him the last hope of ever learning that name. And then a thought came to her.

"Ah well," she thought, "God knows his name."

A few days afterward, John Doe No. 24 was buried in an unmarked pauper's grave. We still don't know John Doe No. 24's name, but you will now know who he was.

He seems to have sprung from the pavement in Jacksonville, Illinois, where the police found him in the early morning hours of 11 October 1945. Of course, he had a life before that day. He had a name and a family before that day. But from that morning until his death, he was simply "John Doe." Only he knew the story of his life before he was found, and he couldn't tell it.

Unable to communicate with the Jacksonville police, he was quickly sent to a courtroom. There, without legal representation, he was found to be, in the quaint but devastating phrase of that day, "feeble-minded." He was sentenced into the nightmarish jumble of the Illinois mental health care system, where he remained for thirty-six years. He was but a teenager at the time and could not have known or understood what was happening to him.

Efforts to learn John's true identity came and went during the forty-eight years he lived after being found in Jacksonville. Several social workers over the years became determined to find out who John was, only to give up after looking in his records and finding nothing.

His fingerprints were taken at the Lincoln State School and Colony in 1947. But there is no evidence of them or reason to believe that they were ever used in an effort to learn John's identity. More than likely, the prints were taken only to help identify him if he were ever pulled, dead, from nearby Salt Creek.

If John's family had reported him missing, but he was not suspected of a crime, giving his fingerprints to a law enforcement agency in 1945 would not have done much good. Missing persons' reports for noncriminals were considered a local matter. There was no national computer database through which the prints could be checked. If the police didn't know where in the country to look for a missing person's report on him, and they didn't, they would not have been able to find his family.

A strong case can be made that John indirectly owed his years of neglect and chlorpromazine-induced stupor in the mental health system to Alexander Graham Bell. Bell, widely regarded as a champion of the deaf, is actually regarded as an enemy by the deaf community. At the 1880 Congress of Educators of the Deaf in Milan, Bell led successful efforts to have sign language banned from schools. Bell was a strong proponent of oralism, which was the movement to force the deaf to speak. Sign language would only have hindered that movement, according to Bell.

The effects of the Milan decision are still being felt at the turn of the millennium and were certainly more profoundly felt in the 1930s and early 1940s, when John would have been most affected. Though sign language existed, John obviously was never taught it as a child. If he had known it and used it when he was first found in Jacksonville, he might very well have ended up in the Illinois School for the Deaf, also in Jacksonville, rather than in the Lincoln State School and Colony. It's especially frustrating to know that John was found so near the School for the Deaf. If he had been taken there, his life would have been much different.

In researching this book, I wondered why, when John was first found, no one wrote questions to him such as, "Where are you from?" The answer apparently is that though he was able to write his name, the "James" or "Lewis" that many people saw him scribble, he could not read. A study by Gallaudet College found that, on average, eighteen-year-old deaf high school graduates in the United States in 1972 were only at a fourth-grade reading level. In 1945, their reading ability was undoubtedly lower.

Kitty Aubry, an instructor at the high school at the School for the Deaf in Jacksonville, has been teaching the deaf since 1970. She explains that it was normal for a deaf teenager in the 1940s to be unable either to understand sign language or to read English.

"The deaf didn't have any power then, and they don't have any power now," she said. "Look at this school. We have over sixty teachers here and are generally considered one of the top three [deaf schools] in the nation. We have only eleven deaf teachers. That's a big number compared to some places.

"I was raised in Michigan, and we were not allowed to sign. The idea was to force oralism. The deaf were going to speak, and they were going to speak right. The incorrect theory was that if they learned how to sign, they would forget how to talk. That's like saying when you learn to swim, you forget how to ride your bike. A. G. Bell was one of the biggest promoters of that. He's viewed now in the deaf heritage texts as one of the greatest enemies of deaf people."

The only way, Aubry says, that John would have known sign language is if he had been a student in a residential school where the language was taught. John may never have attended school at all before he was found in Jacksonville. It is likely that someone earlier in his life had mistakenly diagnosed John as retarded. Federal law stated that retarded children were not required to attend school. If John had been diagnosed as retarded, then that would explain why he could not read when he was found.

The diagnosis of retardation in John's case, while a tragic one, was also not unusual. There are thousands of people who have been diagnosed as retarded when their only problem was a hearing loss.

"I used to go to exit interviews at one of the state facilities in Michigan for the 'mentally deficient,'" says Aubry, "because they finally figured out the people were deaf, so then they'd be released. At the exit interview, the doctors or evaluators discussed the cases. They learned that 'we picked them up because they were waving their hands; we couldn't understand them; we thought they were crazy.'"

Deaf children, says Aubry, are often taught to write their names. But that doesn't mean they can read.

"We don't know if John knew English," says Aubry. "If he did, why didn't he write some sentences down, like, 'I'm deaf. Call an interpreter.' He didn't do that, so that gives us some cause to think he was not successful with English. We also knew he wasn't a success with oralism, or he'd have spoken up. My guess is that he couldn't have known English."

It is almost impossible to believe that John could have understood back in 1945 that he was going to have a commitment hearing or its implications. If no one could learn so much as his name, explaining to him the commitment procedure and his rights under the then-new Illinois law would seem to be out of the question. The rights he was afforded under the state's Revised Mental Health Act, let alone the U.S. Constitution, were of no use to him in that Jacksonville courtroom. His constitutional guarantee of due process, extended by the U.S. Supreme Court to involuntary commitments sixty-two years earlier, was denied him.

From the vantage point offered us by a half century of progress in deaf education and the treatment of the mentally retarded, it's also easy to fault the two doctors and the judge who declared John "feeble-minded" and ended any chance he may have had at a normal life. It's the same with the psychologist in Lincoln who gave John the label "imbecile," a label that stuck with John in one form or another for the rest of his life. But we should not judge them harshly. Their procedures seem as primitive to us as our habit of going to war over oil will someday seem to future generations.

I am intrigued by the two interpretations of the name John was able to write; the name was first thought to be "James" by Bertha Duff and Deputy Tom O'Connell at the Lincoln School and then believed to be "Lewis" in his later years. It appears that John was consistent in the name that he wrote, whether he wrote it in 1945 or 1992.

In John's very erratic cursive writing, "James" and "Lewis" can easily be mistaken for the same name. John's handwriting was not clear. It was a broad scrawl. That being the case, a poorly made *L* could be read as a *J*. And the same mistake can be made with the second letter, reading what is essentially a loop as either an *a* or an *e*. And the third and fourth letters are equally similar to other letters, *m* (or *w*) and *e* (or was it *i*?). In all cases in which his name was written, the last letter was believed to be an *s*. John's name, then, was very likely either James or Lewis. Realizing that those two names are common surnames as well as first names only adds to the riddle.

I believed I had found something important when, in reading the Jacksonville police report from the day on which John was found, I found that the name "George Dunkley" was written in his vest. I contacted the sheriff of Greene County, where John was jailed when he was first found by state policeman Slim Culberth. The sheriff found the record of John's arrest there in 1945. In that record, John was referred to as "George Dunkley." But there was no other clue as to his whereabouts before he was picked up by the Illinois State Police.

In order to find a missing person's report on John, I needed to know where he came from. I guessed that St. Louis would be a logical place to investigate because of its large African American population and its close proximity to the area in which John was first found. I reasoned that John couldn't have traveled far in the light clothes he was wearing when he was found in Jacksonville.

I inquired with the records division of the St. Louis Police Department. I asked if it had a 1945 missing person's report either on a George Dunkley who was never found or on someone matching John's description. It did not.

The vest with the name also hinted at an institution. A school might also put a student's name on his clothes. But if it were John's vest and he came from an institution, why didn't the rest of his clothes have his name on them? When he arrived at the Lincoln School and was issued his clothing, each piece was marked with the name "John Doe No. 2." That was standard procedure at such places.

Conjecturing that John could have run away from some type of institution, I checked with deaf schools and mental hospitals throughout the greater St. Louis area. None of them had a record of anyone matching John's description who had disappeared in 1945. His trail before Slim Culberth picked him up was nonexistent.

The Lincoln State School and Colony during John's first decade there was most assuredly a more violent and nightmarish place than I have described it. Most of the people who lived through it are dead or are walking dead, unable to describe what it was like. The many corpses in the Lincoln School cemetery, were they able, could tell the tale.

What is known of the old Lincoln School—unlicensed doctors practicing on its people, drowned patients dragged from Salt Creek, welfare mothers secreted there to give birth, severely retarded people tied to pillars in the ward called the "Sevens"—is revolting enough. But John's reaction to the hellhole in which he found himself is oddly inspiring. At first, as might be expected, he tried to get out as fast as he could, hence his unsuccessful effort to pry the screens from the windows and his overnight journey to Beason. But it is to his credit that he was able somehow to adjust and even to begin learning at the Lincoln School.

Why didn't he commit suicide when it became clear to him that the Lincoln School was where he would be staying? It would have been an easy enough job, given the lack of supervision and the materials available on a farm. And there was certainly precedent for it. The fact that John survived and even distinguished himself among the patients and staff says much about his spirit.

John had an unexpected drive to achieve. The staff and other patients in Lincoln recognized it. Mary Ransdell sensed it immediately when she met him in Jacksonville. His Springfield group home managers knew it, and so did the staff of the Smiley Living Center in Peoria. They each express their sense of John's spirit in different ways. He earned the respect of other patients and the staff in Lincoln. To Mary, John was a man with a thirst for knowledge and a gentle heart. Later in his life, people saw his spirit through his pantomimed stories of elephants and drunks and through his jokes, such as pretending to read a book. Perhaps this was the purpose of John's life—to illustrate for us again the stunning resiliency of the human spirit.

The first time I spoke with Mary Ransdell, I was made aware of how strong the bond between them must have been. Mary's emotions when discussing the end of their relationship fifteen years earlier were still close to the surface.

Mary was not the first to recognize the spark of intelligence in John, but she was the first to nurture that spark. Once John began to learn from Mary, his life changed as dramatically as it did when he was first taken to the Jacksonville jail. How many times in the thirteen years he lived after leaving her must her memory have come to him?

The things that make life worth living for most people—family, friends, and love among them—were not part of John's life. He had no family for most of his life. He knew only one or two people he could call his friends. He never knew how loving someone can make each day better than it would have been without them. So what made life bearable for John? Cigarettes. Peanuts. Holding a baby. Coffee. Mary Ransdell. Finding a stray coin or a never-opened package of coffee sweetener.

John could be irritable, disagreeable, angry, and even physically aggressive. The less appealing parts of his personality were the more apparent simply because he could never hide them.

While sitting in a Starbucks Cafe in Washington, D.C., singer Mary Chapin Carpenter was reading the *New York Times*. A story about a mysterious man who died in Illinois caught her eye. The story said the man's name was John Doe No. 24.

Carpenter left the cafe, went home, and wrote a song about John. The song, "John Doe No. 24," is included on her compact disc *Stones in the Road*, which has sold over 1.5 million copies. She has also performed the song in concerts in the United States, in Ireland, and throughout Europe.

When she learned that John's grave was unmarked, Carpenter purchased a headstone for him. It is engraved with these lyrics from her song: "life's a mystery, but so too is the human heart."

It was her song that sparked my interest in John. Some initial inquiries found that the record of John's years in the state's care were strictly confidential. I filed a motion with the Morgan County clerk in Jacksonville to have all of John's state records released to me.

Given the fact that no family members of John could ever be found, neither the Illinois Department of Mental Health nor the Illinois Attorney General's Office resisted my motion. At a hearing before Judge J. David Bone in Jacksonville on 13 May 1996, I made my case for obtaining John's records. Judge Bone granted my request. In two weeks, I had the records in my hands. The records included names of people who took care of John, all of the important dates in his life, and information on his medication and his behavior while in the institutions.

From there, finding the story of John's life was a matter of tracking down people who knew him. Luckily, I found two men, Richard Cutts and Lawrence Bussard, who worked at the Lincoln State School and Colony in 1945. Neither man remembered John, but both described the conditions in Lincoln vividly.

I followed John's trail through Lincoln, Jacksonville, New York, Springfield, and Peoria, locating people at each place who helped piece his life together. My interviews, together with John's records and other historical research from the state's mental health agency and the Illinois State Library, are the foundation of this book.

God Knows His Name is a work of nonfiction. The events included here are based on the records and on the accounts of people who were there. In some places, I have re-created events and dialogue and have described John's thoughts. These passages are also based on factual events and interviews. Some of John's emotions, which he expressed during certain events, were recorded by the therapists who worked with him. My descriptions are based on those accounts.

Naturally, with the passage of so many years, there are people who have died who could have shed some light on John's life. None of them, I believe, could have provided any clues to John's true identity.

From the day he entered the Lincoln State School and Colony, any chance for John to live a full life was over, unless years of institutionalization, deprivation, and sadness could be called a full life. During his thirty years in Lincoln, John had no visitors. No one loved John. He never spent Christmas with his family, watched his children grow, or spent a lazy Sunday in a park. He never earned a paycheck, went to his high school prom, or had a date. He left the grounds of the institution in Lincoln once in thirty years. He had one friend. Eventually, when he was probably in his forties, John went blind. He survived all of it. He triumphed over it. He lived. He laughed, and he made other people laugh.

Because of Carpenter's song, millions of people know about John, and as they listen to the song, they wonder how a man could live so long and no one ever know his name. This is the story of how he found a life, if not a name.

In interviewing people from the various stages of John's life for this book, I often thought about what it would be like to see them together in a room, sharing their stories and memories of John with each other. If that were ever to happen, I thought, a much more complete picture of John would be revealed to them and to us. What I have attempted with this book is to put them in that room.

God Knows
His Name

Born into the Arms of the State: Jacksonville, October 1945

God knows his name. Maybe I'll know his name when I get up there to see him.

—Donna Romine, nurse, Peoria, Illinois

Found

Before dawn on Friday, 11 October 1945, Jacksonville, Illinois, police officers Walt Hill and Howard Stout were checking the businesses on the downtown square. It was 5:30 A.M., and they were at the end of their overnight shift. Before clocking out, they took one last cruise through the business district. Everything seemed normal to them. Everything seemed normal most nights in Jacksonville, but this one was exceptionally quiet. The two officers had seen nothing worth reporting all night.

Jacksonville in 1945 was a town of twos—two movie theaters, two city parks, two golf courses, two bowling alleys, two hospitals, 20,000 people, and two small colleges. About 400 students attended Illinois College. The enrollment at MacMurray College was 725, all women.

As the two policemen turned onto Main Street, they noticed someone moving in an alley next to Saner's Tavern. They stopped to investigate and found a young black man rummaging in the alley. He looked to them to be a teenager, but not one they'd ever seen in town before. When the policemen approached him, the youth shook his head and pointed to his ears to indicate that he was deaf. The only sound he made was a grunting, "Uhhh, uhhhh."

When they got a closer look, the officers could see that he was about five feet, six inches tall and weighed maybe 115 pounds. Though the night temperature had dipped into the midforties, he was wearing only a shirt and vest. He carried no identification, but the policemen noticed that his vest was marked inside with the name "George Dunkley."

Of all the places in Illinois in which a deaf man could turn up, Jacksonville was the most desirable. It was home to two state-supported schools for the disabled. One was the Illinois School for the Blind, and the other was the Illinois School for the Deaf. That being the case, it was not unusual to encounter someone on the streets who could neither hear nor speak. But it was very unusual to find someone, either hearing or deaf, in a downtown alley at 5:30 A.M. That being the case, Officers Hill and Stout decided to take their man into custody. Perhaps he was the subject of a missing person's report, or there could be an outstanding warrant for his arrest. As their last act of the night, the officers put him in their squad car, took him to jail, and gave him over to the officers just coming in to start the day shift.

At 8:30 that morning, the Illinois State Police was notified and given his description, along with the name "George Dunkley," which was written on his vest. The Jacksonville Police Department asked the state police if it had a report on anyone with that name or fitting the youth's description who had escaped from either the Lincoln State School and Colony or the Dixon Home—the two state hospitals for the mentally retarded.

At 11:00 A.M., the new prisoner was taken to the Morgan County Jail and put in the custody of Sheriff Earl Hembrough. Sheriff Hembrough assured the city officers that the prisoner would be taken care of until his identity could be learned.

The sheriff looked his new prisoner over. He estimated him to be about sixteen years old. As the youth was booked into the county jail, the clerk put down a tentative "1929?" in the space where the official forms asked for his year of birth. His day and date of birth were left blank.

Half an hour after the young man's arrival at the county jail, the state police called to say that the mystery man was not an escapee from either Lincoln or Dixon. However, he had been picked up by Illinois State Trooper Slim Culberth near East St. Louis on 8 October, three days before he turned up in Jacksonville. Culberth had taken him to the Greene County Jail in Carrollton, where he was booked as George Dunkley. Culberth apparently decided that the name written in the vest was good enough for an identification. The youth was kept for a couple of days, charged one dollar for room and board at the jail, and released on 10 October.

Highway 267 was the main road north out of Carrollton. Thirty miles to the north lay Jacksonville, the only town of any size in the area. Not far to the west of 267 rose the rolling hills that marked the Illinois River. Those hills gave the land its only contour. Otherwise, central Illinois was pool-table flat. The land along 267 consisted of one farm field after another and a few small towns: Belltown, White Hall, Roodhouse, and Murrayville.

A few miles south of Jacksonville, Highway 267 merged with U.S. Highway 67. Once inside the Jacksonville city limits, the highway became Main Street and ran smack in front of Saner's Tavern. If the new prisoner had followed the main highways when he was released from the Carrollton jail, the roads would have led him straight to Saner's Tavern.

The fact that the Jacksonville police officers requested that both state homes for the retarded be checked for escapees indicates that they immediately believed their man was retarded. It was not unusual for the deaf to be judged retarded, only to find out later, sometimes years later, that was not the case.

The authorities in Jacksonville also decided that the name written in the vest was not enough for a positive identification. The vest could easily have been someone else's and could have come into his possession in a number of different ways. During his first day in the Morgan County Jail, the mystery of his identity became deeper.

If the young vagrant's identity could not be discovered, making his return to his family impossible, the School for the Deaf seemed to be the logical place to take him. The school was less than a mile from the county jail. It offered its five hundred students training in marketable skills, including carpentry, cabinetmaking, baking, painting, printing, and millinery work.

But the prisoner was never taken to the School for the Deaf. While in the Morgan County Jail, he masturbated in front of the officers and other prisoners and exposed himself to any women he saw. To the officers, that was simply proof of the earlier suspicion that he was mentally retarded. Once that conclusion was reached, the School for the Deaf was no longer an option. At that time, the school's policy prohibited the admission of anyone regarded as retarded.

Another possibility would seem to have been the Illinois State Hospital for the Insane, which, like the state schools for the deaf and blind, was also in Jacksonville. But state law mandated that the hospital could not admit "feeble-minded persons." The distinction was that the hospital could admit the mentally ill, but not the retarded. The prisoner could not be kept in jail indefinitely, and the authorities were reluctant to simply release him again to resume wandering. Instead, a court hearing was scheduled for his involuntary commitment to a state-run mental institution.

A Revised Mental Health Act had taken effect in Illinois just a few weeks before the young man was found. It included new rules governing involuntary commitment to a mental institution. Most of the new regulations provided for protection for the subject of the commitment, provided that the person was cognizant enough to realize what was happening. It gave the candidates for involuntary commitment, for example, the right to ask for a trial by jury. The jurors would then determine whether the person should be committed. But the person up for commitment, or a guardian or some other representative, had to request a jury trial. Obviously, that meant he or she had to be able to communicate his or her wishes to the court. The young man found in the alley could not communicate with anyone. In accordance with the new law, two physicians were appointed to evaluate the young man's mental state in preparation for his hearing.

On 29 October, eighteen days after he was found, John's case came before Judge Paul Fenstermaker in Morgan County Court. The case was a *Decree in the Case of Feeble-Minded*. The young man with no name had no legal counsel or any representative to speak for him. He may not have even been in the courtroom when his case was heard.

Drs. Tully Hardesty and Albyn Wolfe, who were appointed to evaluate his mental ability, testified that, in their opinion, the prisoner was "feeble-minded." That, coupled with the teen's masturbatory behavior while in custody and the fact that his identity had not been discovered, led Judge Fenstermaker to rule that he should be committed within forty-eight hours to the Lincoln State School and Colony.

He was thereby sentenced by the court to a life that could only fulfill the diagnosis of mental disability the doctors had made. If he were not mentally disabled before he entered Lincoln, simply a warehouse where mental patients were stockpiled by the thousands, he soon would be.

Lost

The county wasted no time in complying with the judge's order. On Tuesday, 30 October, the day after his hearing, the young man found in the alley lost his last hope of returning to his old life. He was instead reborn into a new one. And still, no one knew so much as his name. On that day, Deputy Sheriff Tom O'Connell put the young man in a squad car and drove him seventy miles to Lincoln.

When they arrived, O'Connell led the boy through the doors of the Lincoln School's Male Receiving Cottage. O'Connell showed him a place to sit and then walked to where admissions clerk Bertha Duff was waiting.

"I've got the young boy we found over in Jacksonville," O'Connell told her. "We called you about him. Here are his papers from the judge."

Duff looked them over and peered around O'Connell at John to size him up. O'Connell noticed what she was doing.

"He's a pretty good kid," he said. "He's a good worker if you can make him understand what you want him to do."

Duff nodded to let him know she was listening as she filled out an admission form. "What do we put down for his name?" she asked O'Connell, "just 'John Doe'?"

"That's what we've been calling him," O'Connell replied.

Duff walked over to the new patient and slowly mouthed the words, "What is your name?" He only pointed to his ears and shook his head.

Duff took a piece of paper and a pencil from her desk and handed it to the young man. "What is your name?" she said again, pointing at him and then pretending to write on the paper. "Write your name. Your name. Your name." He wrote something on the paper and handed it back to Duff. "Deputy," she said, "what does that look like to you? It looks to me like it might be 'James.'"

"I can't really tell," O'Connell said as he looked it over. "Maybe 'James.' It could be 'James.' I really can't tell."

"Well," Duff said, "if it looks like anything, it looks like 'James.' But I'm not sure either. It might just as soon be 'jelly.'"

Duff put down her coffee and took up a fountain pen. She dipped it in ink and moved her fingers across the admission form. With those simple motions, she christened the boy "John Doe."

Since there was already another John Doe in Lincoln, Duff gave the new one the name "John Doe No. 2." He would move up to just "John Doe," with no number, in the event that the first one either died while in Lincoln (very likely) or was released (nearly impossible).

Once the admissions form was completed, O'Connell walked over to his charge and extended his hand. O'Connell knew the kind of place his "hard worker" was going to be living in, and he felt a bit sorry for him. Despite the young drifter's episodes of masturbating and exposing himself, O'Connell liked him. He shook his hand and left him to his new life.

Some people are given more than one chance at life. Those who are may choose to re-create themselves into persons who are different from the ones they once were. They renew themselves from the inside out.

But others, like the alley vagrant, have their lives melted down by forces they cannot control. They are remade not by their own choices, but by circumstances, the decisions of others, or twists of fate. And this is how John Doe No. 24 was born.

2 Working Boy: Lincoln, 1945–1955

I'm sorry, I just don't remember him. It's been a long time, and besides, we were just overwhelmed with patients then. I was giving IQ tests constantly. Patients were just coming so fast.
> —Richard Cutts, who administered John's IQ test at the
> Lincoln State School and Colony in October 1945

Forty-Five Hundred to Three

When John and Deputy O'Connell drove through the front gate of the Lincoln School that late October day, the last chance John had of being reunited with his family was gone. That family, wherever it was, would have no way of knowing what had happened to him. If his family members had been searching for him at all, they were using his real name in an effort to find him. Anyone checking arrest or hospital admission records in Illinois would not have found anyone by that name. And his family had no way of knowing that he was now known as John Doe.

The officials in Lincoln apparently cared little about finding out who he was. That wasn't their job. They made no effort. Instead, John was processed through admissions and fed into the machinery of the Lincoln School.

In October 1945, the country was in a postwar state of euphoria. Japan had surrendered on 15 August, after two atomic bombs had been dropped on it. The war was over, and "our boys" were coming home.

Every newspaper in the country was filled with news of the end of the war. Each soldier who came home rated a few paragraphs in the local paper. Sailors were kissing nurses in Times Square. It was a time for celebration, for beginning the Baby Boom with hometown sweethearts and thinking of a future of possibilities for Americans and the peaceful world they had fought to live in. Two days before John was taken to Lincoln, President Harry S. Truman told a crowd in New York's Central Park that "atomic methods of destruction can be definitely and effectively outlawed forever." Americans were looking forward to a long, quiet peacetime.

Just about the time John was found, a doctor removed a soybean from a boy's ear in Glasgow, Illinois. That was front-page news in the Jacksonville newspaper. John's discovery wasn't mentioned.

After John had been formally admitted to the Lincoln School, another patient led him to a supply room where John was given clothes for one day. Each day he would be required to return to the supply room to receive more clothes.

The supply room aide who handed John his clothes wore a white shirt and black bow tie. That was the staff uniform at Lincoln. As John waited, the aide picked out denim overalls, underwear, a T-shirt, socks, shoes, and a blue shirt. That also was the uniform at Lincoln, the patient's uniform.

Regulations required that each piece of clothing be marked with the patient's name. "What's your name?" the supply room employee asked John.

"He's deaf, and they don't know his real name," John's guide replied. "Mrs. Duff said you should just put down 'John Doe No. 2.'"

"Another one?" the aide muttered as he wrote "John Doe No. 2" on each item of clothing. He pointed to the clothes and then to John. "These are yours," he said. In response, John said, "Uhhhhhhh," shook his head, and pointed to his ears. The man mouthed, "Yours, yours," as he pointed back to the clothes and then to John. John picked up his clothes and was led to his room at the receiving cottage. The men's dorm-style rooms were on one end of the building, and the women's rooms were on the other end. A hallway separated the two ends, and all doors leading to the hallway were locked. A nurse was waiting for John in his room.

"This is your bed," she motioned to John. He put his clothes on the bed and looked around.

A receiving cottage was the first stop for all new patients in Lincoln. While there, they received four weeks of physical and mental evaluation. During that time, they were vaccinated for typhoid, scarlet fever, and smallpox. They received one typhoid shot a week for four weeks. If anyone had any serious illness when he or she came in, the theory was that it would become apparent before the patient was mixed into the general population at the end of a month.

Everyone John met at the receiving cottage made signs and gestures at him in an effort to make him understand what he was to do. The signs and gestures were like the popular notion of what Indian sign language must have been—primitive and simple. John had a hard time making any sense of it. When he wasn't being examined or vaccinated, John did nothing. He was not allowed to leave the building.

A week after he arrived, John stood alone at a window. He was upset and angry because he didn't want to be there. He knew only one way to act on what he was feeling. He waited at the window until he saw a woman strolling on the sidewalk outside. John rapped on the window. When she turned toward the sound, he exposed himself.

An attendant working in the cottage was alerted by the noise. "Hey!" he shouted while running toward John, forgetting in the excitement that John was deaf. "Get away from there!"

The attendant grabbed John and pulled him away from the window while John hurriedly refastened his pants. A notation that John Doe No. 2 had exposed his genitals to a woman was the first entry into John's newly begun record.

A few days later, John was back at the window. When no one was looking, he pried at the screen with his fingers. He could see nothing but empty grounds outside. There was no one to stop him from leaving if he could only remove the screen. But he couldn't do it fast enough. Another aide discovered what he was doing and pulled him away again—with a bit more force this time.

"Gotta watch this one," the employee told a nurse. "Make a note to the night staff to keep this guy away from the windows. He either tries to break out every chance he gets, or he drops his pants whenever he sees a woman."

John had realized by now that this was his new home. He didn't want to be in this place. He didn't want to see any more people waving their arms and hands and becoming angry at him when he couldn't understand. He wanted out.

John couldn't have arrived at the Lincoln State School and Colony at a worse time. Even the nineteenth century would have been a better time to be there.

In 1945, the Lincoln School was over its capacity by half and scandalously understaffed. There were forty-five hundred patients and three doctors—one dentist and two psychologists. Normally, there were twelve doctors on staff, but most of them were serving in the war. The other employees, some four hundred of varying capabilities when it came to working with the mentally disabled, were overwhelmed with the numbers of people that just kept coming and the severity of their mental conditions. Lincoln could provide its patients with only the most minimal care.

Illinois had opened its first facility for the treatment of the mentally disabled in 1865. Located in Jacksonville, it was the Experimental School for the Education of Idiots and Feeble-Minded Children. When it opened, it had a grand total of three residents.

In 1871, the Experimental School's name was changed to the "Illinois Institution for the Education of Feeble-Minded Children." Four years later, the name changed slightly again to the "Illinois Asylum for Feeble-Minded Children." Two years after that, the Illinois Asylum was moved to Lincoln.

At first, the Illinois Asylum had as its goal the integration of its residents back into society, mainly by teaching them a trade. Only young people between the ages of six and eighteen who showed potential for becoming self-sufficient were accepted. All of the asylum's residents attended classes. The boys performed manual labor or were taught shoemaking or carpentry. The girls were shown how to perform domestic tasks such as sewing and ironing in the hope that they could be released into a job as a domestic. Students went home to their families for two months in the summer.

In the 1880s, everything changed. By 1883, there were 304 residents in the asylum. Pressure from a prison system unwilling to house prisoners with mental problems forced Lincoln to accept criminals and people of all ages with such severe retardation they would never be able to reenter society. The theory of eugenics, which held that mental retardation was not only inherited but also linked to criminal activity, gained acceptance during this period. Criminals and the retarded were treated alike—both were put away and often, as was the case in Lincoln, in the same place.

In 1910, the Lincoln institution's name was changed again. The "Illinois Asylum for Feeble-Minded Children" became the "Lincoln State School and Colony." The name kept getting better, while the conditions kept getting worse.

The Lincoln School was badly misnamed. To call it a "school" at any time between the turn of the century and the mid-1960s was an outright lie. There was a token school on the grounds, but the majority of its teachers were uncertified and unqualified to teach. It was simply a place where the retarded and other "misfits" could be removed from society and stockpiled. The emphasis in Lincoln was on manual labor, not education and training that would enable the patients to someday leave. Once they were in Lincoln, patients were usually there for life. It was easy to get in, as the courts sent them there by the thousands, but getting out was all but impossible.

Through the 1920s and 1930s, the population at the Lincoln School grew out of control. No other mental hospital in the state would accept the severely retarded or criminally insane. Lincoln's staff was too small to handle the flood of new admissions, and it was neither prepared nor trained to handle the types of people who were coming in. A man arrested for wearing women's clothes was sent to the Lincoln School for evaluation. There was an ordinance in the small town in which he was arrested that prohibited cross-dressing. When asked by the police if he had ever worn women's clothing before, the man replied, "When the pinochle parties I attended were short on female partners."

Preserving the dignity of the resident was way down the Lincoln priority list. Keeping residents from hurting each other, themselves, or the staff was first.

The people in Lincoln ranged from the helpless to the violent. They all lived together, literally within inches of each other. It was so overcrowded that beds were jammed into every available dormitory space, with the head of one bed touching the foot of the other. There was only enough space between the beds for a patient to walk.

There was no privacy and no concept of possessions or personal space. Patients soon lost any sense of self-esteem. The dehumanizing atmosphere in Lincoln ensured that most of the patients would not act in anything like a civilized manner. Treating them like animals led to them behaving like animals. The law of the jungle was the law in Lincoln.

In the 1940s, between seventy and eighty Lincoln residents were so severely mentally disabled that the staff didn't know what to do with them. For these patients, the administration created two wards, the Sevens. Patients were confined in the Sevens from 6:00 A.M. until 8:00 P.M. About half of them simply lay on the floor all day, naked and fouling themselves with their own waste. Others spent the day tied to settees or center support columns in the wards. Screaming and crying could be heard coming from the Sevens all day.

Only one attendant was assigned to the Sevens. He used three other patients for assistance—mostly physical. The only way some of the people living in the Sevens could be quieted was to be pinned to the ground, while their mouths were stuffed with cloth. People who lived in the Sevens were never allowed near windows. They were not allowed to have knives, forks, or spoons. As a result, they ate with their fingers.

The Lincoln School could have been its own town. It had a power plant that manufactured its energy, a farm that produced its food, hospitals in which to treat its sick, a jail to punish its untamable, and a cemetery for the burial of its dead and its secrets.

It was a massive operation: 1,500 pounds of meat, 1,220 gallons of milk, and 200 dozen eggs were consumed each day. Workers mended 347,000 pieces of clothing in a year. Four thousand tons of clothes were washed each year.

The Lincoln School was, appropriately for a mental hospital, schizophrenic. It was part farm, part institution, each a separate entity. The buildings at the institution were standard-issue asylums from a Hitchcock movie: metal beds on stone floors. The one exception was Smith Cottage. Inside Smith Cottage, the rooms were nothing but iron-barred cells, some of them padded. Smith Cottage was jail for the most violent and disruptive patients.

But the farm a few miles to the south of the main institution was home to a large dairy herd, beef cattle, horses, hogs, chickens, corn, wheat, soybeans, truck farms for raising vegetables, a cannery for preserving those vegetables, and, when John arrived, eighteen hundred mental patients.

It would be tempting, and only a small mistake, to say that the animals were treated better than the patients at the Lincoln School farm. But it would be no mistake to say that the animals were more productive than the patients. The dairy cattle, for example, were top of the line, nationally known for their milk production—milk that was processed in the Lincoln School's own pasteurization plant.

The farm was also famous for the amount of corn it produced per acre. Its success was due to the fact that the state of Illinois hired a master farmer and about twenty state employees to oversee the operation. The other reason it was so successful, especially financially for the state, was that virtually all of the labor was done for free by the patients. For years, the farm brought in hundreds of thousands of dollars to the state treasury from the sale of its crops, milk, cattle, and hogs.

The residents of Lincoln who were found fit for work were given as much of it as they could stand. Many of them worked on the farm, but some worked in the residential buildings, taking care of other patients. Whatever their jobs were, they were given the title of "working boy" or "working girl." The terms had nothing to do with age. Every male resident in Lincoln was referred to as a "boy," even if he was forty, fifty, or sixty years old. Staff members also often referred to the patients as "kids."

Working boys and working girls were crucial to the operation of the Lincoln School. They were the ones who milked cows, helped bring in the harvest, cleaned the animals and buildings, served meals, and supervised the residents. The staff at Lincoln was so small, it was unable to keep the place operating without the help of the working boys and girls.

The farm was nothing if not a place of smells—musky, pungent, and pervasive. Eight hundred hogs, three hundred head of cattle, and eighteen hundred men made sure of that. The fact is, when John arrived, Lincoln was much more successful as a farm than it was as a hospital for the mentally retarded.

The Test

On 17 November 1945, the course that the remainder of John's life would take was decided. The day began as he was led into a small room in the receiving cottage. There, he saw a man wearing a suit seated at a table. There was a chair for John directly across the table from the man in the suit. The man rose, pulled out the other chair, and gestured for John to sit down. John didn't know it, but Richard Cutts, one of the staff psychologists at the Lincoln School, was about to test John's intelligence for the purpose of assigning him a job and a place to live.

Dr. Grace Arthur, a Minneapolis psychologist, had designed an IQ test that could be given to people who were deaf. Her Point Scale of Performance Tests relied on visual and manual performance, using puzzles and shapes to test the subject's intelligence. Cutts had a copy of the Arthur test on the table and materials piled on the floor next to him.

John sat down as the man in the suit directed him to do. John had decided that, if this place was going to be his home, he would try his best to be cooperative. So he smiled and nodded at the man in the suit often, hoping to make a friend, a friend who might help him.

Cutts smiled back at John and directed his attention to four wooden cubes before him on the table. Cutts held a fifth cube, with which he tapped each of the four other cubes. He handed the cube to John and motioned for him to do the same. John smiled again and handed the cube back.

"No, no," Cutts said with a shake of his head. He took John's hand that was holding the block and made it touch all four cubes. "See?"

John smiled and nodded. Cutts took the cube back again, touched all four cubes, and then touched the third one again.

"Can you do that?" he asked John as he offered him the cube. Cutts pointed to the cube and to John. "Can you do it?" he asked again.

John tapped one cube and handed the original one back to the man.

"No," Cutts said and shook his head again for visual emphasis. He motioned again to the cubes on the table. "Touch all four, see, and then back to the third cube."

This time he guided John's hand to the correct cubes, just to get him started. He guided him again and then a third time. Then he let John tap the cubes by himself.

But as the test went on, it became more complicated. Cutts touched cubes 1, 2, 3, 4 and then 2 again; 1, 4, 3, and 2; 1, 4, 2, and 3; 1, 3, 2, and 4. He continued the sequences, each time handing John the cube to duplicate what he had just done. Eventually, John was able to complete one sequence of five taps, but then Cutts was tapping a series of six cubes, and John couldn't remember which order they were in.

"OK," Cutts finally said. "Let's just move on." He put the blocks away, pulled a puzzle from a pile on the floor, and laid the board and pieces on the table. There were eight pieces: a star, a circle, a cross, a diamond, a semicircle, a square, a triangle, and a rectangle. Cutts put the shapes into three piles. At the upper right corner of the board, he stacked the star, the diamond, and then the circle. At the center, he put the cross, the hexagon, the semicircle, and, on top, the square. Then, at the upper left corner, he put the oval, the triangle, and then the rectangle.

John looked at the shapes, but his attention was really focused on the man across from him. He sensed something that made him realize this man was important.

"All right, John," Cutts said as he motioned for John to look at the stacks. "You see these pieces? Put them in the correct spaces in the puzzle." He moved a piece toward the puzzle. "See?" John indicated that he understood. He didn't, but he wanted this man to know that he was willing to do what he asked.

But Cutts had another problem. This part of the test consisted not only of putting the puzzle pieces in the correct spaces but also of judging John on how quickly he could do it—if he could do it at all. Cutts had to make John understand that he had to work as fast as he could. But the test manual warned that the subject shouldn't be hurried so much that he did a sloppy job. This direction of hurrying, but not too much, was a subtlety that John couldn't grasp.

Back in Minneapolis, Dr. Arthur's deaf test subjects had a common sign for "fast." The sign was making a fist and flicking the thumb upward. But this wasn't Minnesota, and for all Cutts knew, the Minnesota deaf sign for fast could be the Illinois deaf sign for flipping a coin. So Cutts pointed to his watch. By this, John was supposed to know that he was to work quickly. John thought the man in the suit wanted him to see his watch.

Cutts decided that, for his part, he would follow the manual's instructions. John would score what he would score. Cutts looked at his watch and raised his hand.

"Ready." He gave John an encouraging look. "Go!" He dropped his hand. John didn't move, but he did smile and give a small wave back to the man in the suit as he thought the man had just done to him. He did want to be friendly.

The instructions called for John to put the eight puzzle pieces in their places three times. Each time he was to be encouraged to do it faster. John was only able to put a few of the pieces into the puzzle but did it slowly.

After putting the puzzle away, Cutts rose from his chair, crossed the table, and turned John's chair around so that John's back was to the table. While John was not looking, the doctor arranged the next puzzle. The test's instructions specified that the subject should not get a chance to see the pieces before this particular puzzle test began.

John was nervous as he sat with his back to the table. He wondered what the man was doing. He wanted this game to be over. He had tried to do what the man in the suit wanted, but he sensed that he was not doing it right.

When John was turned around, he saw on the table before him a wooden cutout of a male mannequin. Scattered around it were his arms, legs, and head. Cutts motioned to the pieces and the body. John immediately put the head where it belonged. But then he stopped. He studied the arm and leg pieces. They looked similar. Were these the arms, or were these the legs? He put one leg in an arm socket and an arm where the leg should be. Then he noticed that the legs had shoes on the ends of them. He put the legs below the waist but had them on the outside of the body, not in the hip sockets where the legs would fit. He looked at the man in the suit for some approval, but Cutts was already arranging the next test.

The Arthur test was designed to take from forty-five minutes to an hour to complete, but John and Cutts were going to go on longer than that. It took time for Cutts to explain the directions in a way John could understand. John was still unsure and took his time with everything.

Cutts cleared the mannequin puzzle away and turned John away from the table again. Cutts laid a board on the table. The board had holes shaped like three circles and a cylinder. Above the board were twelve different shapes, some of which fit together into circles, and some of which fit into a cylinder. John had five minutes to arrange the pieces correctly so that they fit the holes. He didn't finish in five minutes, but he had completed a couple of the circles when his time was up. It was his best performance so far, but he didn't know it. John was frustrated and angry. He decided that none of the things he was doing had any value. He no longer wished to please Cutts. But there were more tests to do.

The next puzzle board showed a scene with two horses in a field. The horses had no legs or heads. A few pieces of the background were also missing. All of the missing pieces were lying at the top of the puzzle. This was another timed test. John put the horses together, but the background was confusing to him. He was still trying to figure it out when the man in the suit motioned for him to stop.

The final test was a maze. Despite Cutts's efforts, John couldn't understand what he was supposed to do with the pencil and the lines on the paper. John simply doodled on the paper. He couldn't have known that he was losing IQ points simply for lifting his pencil from the paper as he made his lines and shapes. But that was part of scoring the test. He was happy when the man in the suit finally indicated that he could go back to his room.

John learned a great deal while he took his IQ test, but nothing that he learned had anything to do with the score he would receive. He saw books on the shelves of the room, and, though he couldn't read, he wanted to remember that those books were there because he liked looking at pictures. He learned that being nice to people didn't mean that he was going to be treated any better than he had already been. He learned that putting puzzles together was not necessarily much fun. He learned that spinning hands meant "fast," but he also knew that tomorrow there would be a different man in a suit who would use a new set of signs and gestures. He learned that people would go to great trouble to try to communicate something to him, and he would be glad to cooperate with them if he only could understand what it was they wanted. He learned that the signs and gestures that he had already learned before he was found in Jacksonville were no good to him because whenever he used them with the people in this place, they didn't understand him.

On 28 November, the staff at the receiving cottage met to decide John's future. Dr. Isidore Walters, the physician in charge at the receiving cottage, was in charge of the meeting. Dr. Walters was born in Russia and spoke with a thick accent. That inspired the staff to call him "Dr. Val-tairs." Given the American-Russian tensions that were beginning to increase, the staff often wondered where his heart was—with Truman or with Stalin. Whenever the doctor's hunched figure was seen walking around the Lincoln grounds, he was never without his briefcase. Inside his briefcase were two items: a pipe and tobacco.

The doctor did not have a medical license, and he had not practiced medicine for years. He got into the field by being apprenticed to a doctor when he was young. He was simply "grandfathered in" when the regulations for practicing were instituted. At any rate, doctors didn't need a medical license to practice at a state mental hospital.

Dr. Walters had been running a drugstore in New Holland when the war began. But Lincoln was desperate for medical help during the wartime shortage and hired him.

"John Doe No. 2," said Dr. Walters, "was committed here by a Morgan County judge. He has no family that we know of, and we don't have any way of finding any. As a result, we have no family medical history on him. We have no history at all. He was just wandering around the streets over in Jacksonville and was picked up by the police.

"He doesn't look to be too well fed. When he came to us, he weighed 120 pounds. He is about five foot, six inches tall. I'd say he's around the age of eighteen. He can walk, and he can see but is deaf. He is able to toilet himself. But, as far as talking goes, he cannot speak at all, but he can make sounds. He seems to understand some of the signals we give him. Mr. Cutts, how about his mental ability?"

"Based on the results of the Arthur Point Scale of Performance Test," Cutts said, "I rate his IQ at forty-three. He has a mental age of six years and ten months, which, for a sixteen or eighteen year old, puts him in the upper imbecile category. He cooperated well in the test. Apparently, he is illiterate but seemed to understand my instructions fairly well."

"I note that his behavior on the ward is not satisfactory," continued Dr. Walters. "He is destructive and tries to remove screens from windows, apparently in an attempt to escape. It is reported that he frequently engages in sexual perversion, such as masturbatory activities and exposing himself to women."

The evaluation meeting broke up with Dr. Walters saying he would come to a placement decision soon. On 1 December, Dr. Walters was in his office, going over the reports on the men in the receiving cottage and officially assigning them to their places inside Lincoln. He knew immediately what to do with John.

First of all, there were the results of John's IQ test. He had Cutts's evaluation of "imbecile" and the recorded incidents of John exposing himself and trying to pry the window screens away.

Dr. Walters relegated John to the bottom of the Lincoln sludge pile. He sent John to live at the farm, where the most profoundly handicapped people in Lincoln were assigned. It was the worst of the worst.

The IQ test that John very likely thought was some kind of recreational game with puzzles, blocks, and mazes was instead the blueprint for his life in Lincoln.

High Brows and Low Grades

Residents at the farm lived in what were referred to in Lincoln, in a fit of misplaced optimism, as "cottages." The name inspired an image of a rustic home with a white picket fence and brightly painted shutters. The reality was something different. The farm cottages were E-shaped buildings. The design was meant to be functional, with dormitory areas at both the top and the bottom of the E and a day room in the middle. John was assigned to Farm Cottage 7 with about one hundred other men.

The farm in the 1940s had much in common with a medium-security prison. The residents were allowed to roam the grounds, sometimes unsupervised, as did prison trustees. The lives of both patients and inmates were regimented and scheduled. Everything was decided for them, including the clothes they wore, the meals they ate, when they ate them, and how they spent their time.

Another characteristic the farm shared with a prison was that the sexes were strictly separated. There were no women residents at the farm when John arrived. The men and women were kept apart, even after death. In the Lincoln School's cemetery, the men were buried in their own rows, and the women in theirs.

The 1,800 men at the farm lived together in such close proximity that homosexual activity among them was inevitable, especially at night when each cottage had 100 to 150 residents in their beds and usually only one or two employees to watch them.

But there was one odd twist to the homosexually inclined atmosphere at Lincoln that would never have been allowed in a prison. Lincoln's residents had formed their own dance band. Some knew how to play instruments when they were admitted, and others picked it up while inside. Whenever the patient band performed at a dance, the men who wanted to dance were allowed to dance only with other men. They held each other and shuffled along to the strains of big band music.

Just as prison inmates have a hierarchy, with child molesters at the bottom, the patients at Lincoln had their own caste system. For several reasons, John was quickly relegated to its lowest depths. The state's opinion that John was severely retarded was one factor that made him an outcast among the other patients. Even though most of the residents were retarded, some were more retarded than others. As a result, a class system had developed along the lines of who was more retarded than whom. The residents split into two camps: "high brows" and "low grades." The low grades were the most severely retarded and the most abused.

Though the patients separated themselves into the two categories, Lincoln also had an official system of classifying its patients. Their records showed that they were either "idiots, imbeciles, high-grade mental defectives, borderlines, dull-normals, or of average intelligence."

Besides being called a "high brow" or a "low grade," every resident had a nickname. John was called "Dummy," as were all of the others who couldn't speak. The staff and the other residents called John by that name. Not being able to hear that was very likely one of the only times John's deafness was a blessing. Otherwise, his inability to communicate dropped him further down the scale.

Another major disadvantage for John was, as they put it in the vernacular of the Lincoln School, "He didn't have no people." Having "no people" meant he had no relative or friend on the outside to whom he could complain, no matter how bad the conditions were or how much he was mistreated. The staff knew that and likely took advantage of it. He also had no one to send him money, gifts, or food from home, which the other patients used to bribe the staff into giving them special considerations.

Even the very name they gave him, "John Doe," worked against him. It was a synonym for nobody. He shared his name with every lonely, unknown corpse who ever turned up in a city morgue. It appeared on thousands of official forms on which something had to be written in the space for "name." John Doe, Anytown, USA. Respect was hard to come by for a man with no name who came from nowhere and had no one.

The fact that John was black also put him on the lowest step. As a rule, black residents at Lincoln were given the most menial jobs and the harshest treatment. Their living areas were segregated by race as much as possible in a place where people were crammed so tightly together. Even the residents' parents' association was affected. When the parents came to Lincoln for their annual meeting, the blacks could only stay in certain hotels.

Dr. Walters decided that John was too small and too severely retarded for farm work. Instead, John was told to put napkins inside napkin rings until another job could be found for him.

As soon as John's living arrangements were decided, he was driven the few miles down Route 66 from the receiving cottage to the farm. Driving through the entrance to the farm, the first thing John noticed was the mass of people—eighteen hundred of them for the twelve residence cottages.

Patients, almost all of them dressed in overalls, were walking everywhere he looked. Some of them led a small herd of cattle down a path between residence buildings. It appeared as if the surrounding corn and bean fields had broken through the Lincoln School fences.

John was taken to his dormitory-style room at Farm Cottage 7. The building's attendant was Maggie Nance, a short, feisty woman dressed in white. She led him inside and showed him where his bed was located and where the bathroom was. She looked him over gratefully, figuring anyone only five feet, six inches tall wouldn't be too hard to handle.

A working boy took John outside to show him around. Since it was early in December, the fall harvest was finished. The fields that had been jammed with brown corn stalks were now bare. Cattle walked their slow, leaden walk through the frozen mud in the fields. Here and there, chickens scattered in the sun. John took in all of the farm's sights and, especially, its smells. When he was taken back to the cottage, he understood that this was where he would be living.

As he looked over his new home, he was unaware that people were checking him out as well. Other residents were sizing him up. They were in agreement with Maggie Nance. Anyone only five feet, six inches tall wouldn't be too hard to handle.

Lincoln was a violent place. Some patients had won hard-earned reputations for being tough. They attacked each other, and they fought with the employees. The building attendants quickly learned which patients were prone to violence and, also, which ones were good at it. One of the better punchers was called "Chicago Joe" to differentiate him from the many other Joes living at the farm. Chicago Joe was a big man and an experienced fighter, and it often took several people to wrestle him to the ground. Another patient, Elliot, wasn't much of a fighter but had a particular talent for teasing low grades until they either broke out in tears or attacked him.

One of the Lincoln patients was given the nickname "Kitty Cat." He earned that name by the way he fought, with fingers outstretched to scratch his victim's eyes. He attacked his victims with his "claws" raised, like a cat.

John had not been living in Cottage 7 very long when three patients approached his bed as he slept in the darkness. The first one jumped on him and began to pound his face. Startled awake, John cried out.

The first patient covered John's mouth to stifle his cries, while another pounded his body with his fists. John didn't understand what was happening. Who was doing this? Why? His shouts and the commotion could be heard in the nearby beds, but no one came to help him.

The third attacker grabbed John's crotch and squeezed it hard. The pain and pounding brought John to tears. He made inhuman sounds and could not fight back, but the beating went on and on. He tried to struggle but could barely move under the weight of all three men.

Down the hall, Maggie Nance read a magazine, as oblivious to this beating as she had been to others so many times before. As long as the patients were quiet . . .

Blood ran from John's nose and mouth as he struggled to protect himself. Finally, his attackers grew tired of pounding on him. Their message for John had been sent. It was over for now, and they went back to their beds, exhilarated by the blood and the release of their aggression. John curled himself painfully into a fetal position. He cried until he finally found sleep.

In the morning, an attendant on the day shift came to get the men in line for breakfast. He saw John's blood-caked face and noticed that he had difficulty in walking. "What happened?" the worker gestured to him. John made fists, simulated hitting himself, and pointed to nearby patients. The employee turned to a group of them who were getting dressed. "What happened to this boy?" he asked them. Some laughed. Others said nothing, only continued putting on their clothes. No one saw anything. No one knew anything.

John was sent to an infirmary nurse for treatment, and a brief report was filed. Though no one was talking, the staff had a pretty good idea what had happened. The same thing always happened to the new patients. Some of the staff members said, quietly, that someone should have known this was coming, and a closer eye should have been kept on John his first nights in the cottage.

The beatings continued in different intensities and with different numbers of patients involved and at different times of the day. John was unable to sleep much for fear of being attacked. Sometimes he was waiting for them and put up a token fight. But someone of his size was no match for most of the others, especially when two or more ganged up on him. Sometimes they took him by surprise. Either way, he never had much of a chance to defend himself.

One week after he was sent to the farm, John became convinced nobody could help him and nobody was going to take him home. He didn't want to be beaten up anymore. He tried to escape that night. Nance noticed he was missing at 7:45. She estimated he could have been gone forty-five minutes by then. John never found his way off the grounds in the dark. It was probably for the best. It turned out to be the coldest night of the month—six degrees above zero.

Because of his escape attempt, he was reassigned to Farm Cottage 3 as punishment. Farm Cottage 3 had more severely retarded patients and was even more crowded than Cottage 7. But, to John, the move to 3 was no punishment. In the new building, as bad as it was, the beatings were not as frequent. To his delight, John found that he could hold his own with the more retarded patients in a fight. And more than that, he was becoming good at it.

Escape

By his fourth month in Lincoln, John had gained fifteen pounds on state food. His physical improvement led the staff to decide he was fit for doing something other than putting napkins in napkin rings.

One morning, instead of being led to his usual job in the dining room, John was told to follow a working boy to a new assignment. John was led down the hall from the dining room to the day room in Cottage 3. Each cottage had a day room. It was a great hall filled during the day with men who were too severely disabled to be working boys. The men were taken to the day room in the morning and left there. Some of the catatonic patients were literally dumped on the floor. The residents stayed there, doing nothing, all day, every day. This was as good as life in Lincoln ever got for them.

As the working boy led John into the day room, it was still early in the morning. Not many people had arrived. It was nearing spring, 1946, and the windows were open so that some air could pass through and disperse the smell that lingered even when no one was there. The attendants were officially in charge of the day room. They enlisted working boys to help them control the others and to do the dirty jobs the attendants didn't want to do. If their working boys had to resort to their fists to keep order, so be it.

The working boy who would be John's boss in the day room handed him a mop and gestured to him that he was to clean the terrazzo floor. Cleaning the floor was a common occupation for low-grade working boys. It took some time to complete and kept them busy for a while. Cleaning the floor was also used as a form of punishment. Patients who broke the rules or who simply got on someone's bad side were assigned to pull heavy wooden blocks wrapped in towels along the floor, shining it until their boss could see his face in it.

As John was working on the floor, more people came in. As they did, John found it impossible to keep his mind on what he was doing. The day room began to fill with men. They were lined up in rows by the other patients who brought them there. Some were sitting in cane-backed wheelchairs. Some were lying in beds.

John saw a man contort his body into an impossible posture, his eyes staring into nowhere. John turned around and saw two staff members wrestling with another man, putting him in a chair and holding him down as they bound his arms and legs. The man's mouth was open in a scream John could not hear. John tried to not look, but he couldn't turn away. Another man slid out of his chair and fell to the floor. People stepped around him and on him. Another one was dropped onto the floor as he was brought in. Another man hit himself in the face as he paced back and forth, back and forth, back and forth. If the staff members saw it, they didn't let on.

John was interrupted by a tap on his shoulder. He turned to see the patient who brought him there gesturing for him to follow. He took his mop and walked, happy to have something to take his mind off what he was seeing. The man led John down a row of people, some of whom grabbed for John, but he twisted away.

"Here, clean this with your mop." The man pointed at John and his mop, then at the floor. John looked down and saw a man lying in his own vomit. He had a brown streak of feces on his pant leg. The smell rising from him was overpowering.

John turned to run, but the other man caught him, powerfully jerked him back, and held him tight so that John couldn't move. John knew what he was supposed to do but couldn't bear it. Tears came to his pleading eyes, and he shook his head no. John made sounds that the other man couldn't understand. The more John resisted, the angrier the other working boy became. John took a slap from him, hard and in the face. He shouted at John, "Clean it up, goddamn you, goddamn low grade!" John didn't have to hear to know. He refused again.

The next blow was a punch in John's face. John was turned away and down from its force. The other man grabbed John's arm, forced the mop into it, and pointed to the mess on the floor. An attendant had arrived to help force John to do the job. Together, they grabbed John's arms and forced him to his knees in the vomit.

They rolled the patient away from the mess with their feet. John, moaning all the while, did what they made him do. He cleaned it this time and the next time and the next time, and it eventually became easier.

As the days went by, John was made to understand that his job was to watch the people in the day room, make sure they didn't hurt themselves, and clean up their messes without being told. This was his job every day, beginning after breakfast and ending at dinner.

John understood. He understood more than anyone in Lincoln knew—and he made up his mind. When the weather turned warmer, he would run away.

Salt Creek ran by the eastern edge of the farm. Patients were taken to the creek often for fishing trips or to walk along its banks. John had been there several times already with residents and staff. But when he was there, he was doing something other than fishing. He was looking. The attendants with his group noticed, but they thought he was just wandering away and brought him back several times.

John noticed that there was no fence on the creek side of the Lincoln School. The rest of the school was surrounded by a fence. But water was the only barrier that kept patients from escaping to the east.

John didn't find what he was looking for his first day at the creek. It took several trips before he finally saw it. When he did, he knew that this was the night he would go. The day was 5 March.

At about 6:30 P.M., dinner was over, and the 150 men in Cottage 3 were already preparing for bed. John knew that it was the most chaotic time of the day. Some patients were in the bathroom, and some were sitting on their beds calling for help. It was the perfect time to escape. There were two male attendants on duty that evening. John waited until one attendant was busy helping someone at the other end of the room. The other was in the bathroom. John simply walked out the door.

Once outside, he headed for Salt Creek. He kept looking around as he moved between the buildings, but he could see no one. He knew that there could be a crowd making noise just around the next building, and he wouldn't be able to hear it. But he also knew that almost everyone was inside getting ready for bed. Every cottage was as chaotic as his. He began to run. When he passed the last cottage, he almost cried out with joy, but he stopped himself. He knew he had to be quiet.

He reached the creek, scrambled through the trees and down the bank. He walked quickly along the edge to the spot he had found earlier in the day. Salt Creek had deep pools, especially in the spring when the water was high. But it also had shallow crossings. Someone who knew what he was looking for could get across.

It was dark, and John kept looking. He wondered if he had gone the wrong way. He thought about turning around and looking in another direction. But he kept going. Suddenly, there it was, a sandbar breaking the water. John knew what that meant—shallow water. He had seen staff members and other patients wading out there earlier that day and noted exactly how shallow it was.

On average, the Lincoln School pulled one dead patient a year out of Salt Creek. Some of the more seriously retarded inmates who tried to escape just plowed into the water and kept going as it got deeper. Others pitched forward in shallow water and couldn't get up or raise their heads. Some who drowned in the creek weren't even escaping. Their attendant just lost track of them for a bit, and they were dead. All of them were buried in the Lincoln School cemetery, and nobody ever knew the details.

John walked carefully into Salt Creek, not quite sure of himself. He was afraid. It had been a wet February, and the creek was running faster than normal. When the water crested over his knees, he became more frightened, and this time he couldn't stop himself from crying out. But he had to keep moving. Drowning was better than going back.

His feet soon found the sandbar. He climbed up it, out of the water for a few steps and then back in. It wasn't as deep on the other side—just midway up his calves. He climbed up the far bank and didn't look back.

All that lay ahead of him was open, flat farm fields. Tractors had not yet worked the ground in preparation for planting season. That meant huge chunks of mud that hadn't been broken up by the plows. The chunks made walking treacherous and tiring. When John had gotten far enough away that he could no longer see the lights of the Lincoln School power plant behind him, he sat in the mud and cried tears of joy and fear. For a long time, he just sat there, resting and breathing the air of freedom.

He was missed about twenty minutes after he'd gone. Wallace and Clark, the attendants at Farm Cottage 3 that night, were ready to turn out the lights in the dorm when they saw the empty bed.

"Whose bed is that?" Wallace asked his partner.

"I don't know. We're going to have to look it up," Clark replied.

It took a few minutes to find it.

"John Doe No. 2. Shit," said Wallace.

Wallace picked up a phone at his desk and called Dr. William Carroll, the physician in charge that night. "Dr. Carroll, this is Clark on FC3. I've got a damn patient missing. John Doe No. 2, the deaf guy who can't talk. I don't know. It gets so damn hectic over here when I'm trying to get them to bed. Arthur couldn't get his pants off, and I had to help him, and I guess . . . Jesus, we can't keep track of them all. Right. OK."

Dr. Carroll called the Illinois State Police just after 7:00 P.M. to report that John was missing. He told the dispatcher that police should look for a "colored male, very black, wearing dark blue shirt and pants." He told him John very likely couldn't function on his own.

As usual, the first place the staff looked was in Salt Creek. They expected they would find John floating in it somewhere. But by that time, John had begun to walk again. He could see a highway about a mile to his left. There was only farmland ahead and to his right. He didn't want to get too close to the highway for fear someone would see him, so he stayed in the muddy fields and kept going ahead, keeping the highway a good distance to his left.

He could see the lights from several farms in the distance. He picked the closest one and headed for it, keeping his eye on the light pole in the farmyard as a guide. He frequently fell over clods of mud in the dark but kept picking himself up and moving on. He didn't know how long he had been walking by the time he reached the farm. He didn't even know where he was going. He just wanted to be gone.

He looked through the windows of the house and saw a man in a chair, reading the newspaper. John looked for a dog in the yard. He knew most farms had a dog, and if it put up a ruckus, he'd be caught for sure. He didn't see one. He walked carefully to the barn, happy to be out of the mud. He sat against one wall to rest.

He took quick stock of himself, and he was a mess. His boots were saturated and full of mud from the creek bottom. He pulled them off and took off his socks to dry them out. His feet ached from walking on the uneven ground. His pants were slathered with mud from the thighs down. His thoughts were jumbled. He saw the day room in his mind and the people reaching out for him and worse, until he wanted to think about it no more.

He slid down the barn wall into the cool grass and quickly fell asleep. As he slept, the light from inside the farmhouse clicked off.

John hadn't slept well since he came to Lincoln. Most of the time he was afraid to fall asleep. This night, he slept soundly. Nearby, on Highway 10, the highway John had seen, patrol cars searched the darkness for him. Back at Salt Creek, a few working boys waded in, looking for his body.

John was up and moving again before the sun. He kept walking in the same direction as he had the night before, always keeping the highway on his left. The mud quickly clung to his shoes, still wet from the day before. The shoes were tight, making it harder for him to walk. Whenever he found a stout stick, he sat down to scrape away the mud that lined his shoes. A few steps later, they'd be caked again.

He was hungry as the sun began to rise, but he didn't know how to get anything to eat. He walked straight for the rising sun. No one was working in the fields, so it was easy for him to travel on, unnoticed.

At about midmorning John saw a town up ahead. He was so hungry, he decided he would go there and try to find food. Maybe he could work for it. Maybe someone would just give him some.

A deaf, mute black man covered with mud drew immediate attention in Beason, Illinois, the town John walked into on the morning of 6 March. He had made it about nine miles away from the Lincoln School—not nearly far enough to avoid going back. The townspeople of Beason knew immediately where he had come from; they knew it even before the town cop arrived to hold him for the state police. People in Beason were used to seeing escapees from the Lincoln School. The men who turned up there usually didn't cause any trouble, but most people were leery of them anyway.

John was in the hands of the police minutes after he arrived in town. The state police cars arrived soon after that, and Dr. Carroll was quickly notified that his man was in custody. John was sitting in the county jail back in Lincoln when an attendant arrived to take him back to the farm.

As soon as John saw the man, he knew it was over. He knew he was going back to that place. Until then, he had held out some tiny hope that he would end up somewhere else. He knew now he could never get away. It was the last time he ever tried.

Back at the Lincoln School, John was put in rompers, a kind of jump suit with short pants. He was forced to wear them for a few days as part of his punishment for escaping. Wearing rompers humiliated the patients. The theory was that it would be a deterrent to their misbehaving. Having the troublemakers in rompers made it easier for the staff to keep track of them. And, as extra punishment, another job was added to John's day room work. He was given toilet-cleaning duty.

Albert

John soon started smoking cigarettes, as most of the other men in Lincoln did. The state supplied patients with tobacco, a poor grade of it that was processed by prisoners at the Menard state penitentiary in Chester. Patients were frequently given free pouches of the prison tobacco. Cigarette papers were handed out for free at the commissary, and the patients rolled their own. Smoking was one of their few pleasures. Smoking or not, life would have been intolerable for John had he not eventually made a friend.

Albert was from a large Catholic family in Chicago. He was born in the 1930s. When the Depression hit, his father was dead, and his mother realized that she couldn't support a big family alone. She heard about the Lincoln State School and Colony but misunderstood its purpose. She believed it to be an actual school in which the students were supported by the state. She thought that sending one or two of her children there would be a way out from under so much responsibility. She went to court and had Albert and his brother committed—easy to get in, all but impossible to get out.

Albert was a normal three-year-old when he went into Lincoln. But in Lincoln Albert became a person whom mental health professionals term "environmentally handicapped" from neglect. When he was old enough, he became a working boy, mainly in the kitchen areas. He received no schooling of any kind outside of the kind of street education living in the Lincoln School provided. The Lincoln version of street smarts was more appropriately termed "system smarts" in that patients learned to work the system to their advantage. They learned the important things they needed in order to survive. For example, they learned which attendants were prone to use their fists on them and which ones were softer touches.

Albert and John were close in age. They were both black, and they were both low grades. There weren't many other people at Lincoln who would have anything to do with either of them. John and Albert worked out a system of communication between them that only they understood. They could often be found during their free time, walking or sitting together, flashing their signs and signals back and forth in conversation.

Each year in the 1940s, the Lincoln School sponsored a Summer Festival. The Summer Festival was a chance for the school to throw the doors open to about two thousand visitors—parents and Lincoln town residents— and put on a show for them. Aside from its dance band, the Lincoln School had a drum and bugle corps that once won awards at the Illinois State Fair. It also had a kazoo band comprised of farm residents who couldn't play any other instrument. With the bands and parades and tours that they gave, the school put on an impressive festival. The Summer Festival was always a good occasion to invite dignitaries to see Lincoln at its best.

One year, the festival had an international theme. Patients wore the costumes of various countries. They paraded through the grounds wearing their costumes and carrying signs identifying which countries they represented. It was as if it were modeled after the opening march in the Olympic Games.

Wonderful things didn't happen often in the Lincoln School. There was little beauty or anything to inspire the patients to awe. Simply catching a fish in Salt Creek was, for many of them, an occasion to be remembered and recalled for years afterward. But there was something in Lincoln that touched John's soul with a joy that even forty years later had not died.

George Treatch played the trumpet. In the late 1920s, he joined a band and traveled the upper Midwest, playing dance music in small clubs. It was a rugged life, traveling winter and summer. He and his bandmates once burned their sheet music to keep warm while traveling in a bitter South Dakota winter. They said later that if they had to sacrifice something, the sheet music was the most logical because they already knew their parts.

Treatch was from Galesburg, about seventy miles west of Lincoln. He came to Lincoln in 1941 to lead its Maple Club Band. Five years later, he became the band director at the Lincoln School. He found some musical talent among the patients there, enough talent to build a 120-piece marching band. Once he learned the limitations of his players, he wrote them musical arrangements that corresponded with their abilities. When he went on vacation for two weeks, he came back to find that everything had been forgotten. He had to rehearse the band members as if they were seeing the music for the first time.

He wasn't only the band leader; he was nursemaid, policeman, etiquette instructor, and counselor. Treatch knew that people in the towns where the band marched would be skeptical about its professionalism. He wanted to make sure that the band's behavior, as well as its playing, was impeccable. The band members, outfitted in their trademark red coats, marched in thirty-five or forty parades a year. They played a concert for the governor in Springfield and for other state institutions.

From the marching band, Treatch spun off thirty or forty members into a dance band. Nearly every week, the band would play for the patients at the main institution. Occasionally, it played a dance at the farm.

The patients who were crawling on the ground first caught John's attention. He had seen groups of patients walking somewhere in rows but hadn't thought anything of it. But then he saw several low grades incapable of walking who were crawling after the others. He watched people being pushed in wheelchairs, all of them going in the same direction. Soon, a working boy motioned for John to fall in line with the others from his farm cottage. They joined the flow toward some unknown destination. Most of those who couldn't walk were being carried by working boys. But there were those few who had no one to help them, so they crawled.

Ahead, John could see that the line of people was going into the gymnasium. He had been in the gym for exercise periods and to watch pickup basketball games between the working boys. But when he entered this time, the gym was transformed. A makeshift stage had been erected on the wooden basketball court. Folding chairs were placed in rows. As the patients in wheelchairs arrived, they were lined up on one side of the stage. And on the stage was George Treatch and the dance band, sitting behind colorful music stands painted with a bright "LSS" for Lincoln State School.

The band members were dressed in white shirts, dark ties, and black pants. There were a few women in the band in white blouses and dark skirts. All of the musicians sat quietly, waiting for the crowd to arrive. The lights of the gym glinted off their brass instruments: trumpets, trombones, and saxophones. Treatch was a brass man all the way and would not allow strings, not even a guitar, in his dance band.

John sat in one of the folding chairs, eyes full of wonder at the scene before him. He saw the same people he saw every day in the day room, but he had never seen them like this before. They were excited and anticipating something special. A vibration in the air made John's stomach feel light. What is music to a deaf man? On this night, it was everything.

When Treatch's band struck up the first low notes of "Tenderly," John knew it. His sternum buzzed with each note. He could see the happiness on the hearing people's faces. He saw smiles of people whom he had only seen in tears or in anguish. He was transfixed by the way the instruments caught the light as they moved. He couldn't stop staring at them.

Soon, one or two pairs of men began to dance with each other. John moved closer to the stage so that he could feel the vibrations from the music more intensely. The band played popular tunes of the day: "Take Me," "I Can't Get Started," "When You're Smiling," and "It's the Talk of the Town." John knew nothing of the names of the songs or the bands that had made them popular. But he could feel the changing tones of the music in his bones.

A man he had seen in his farm cottage approached him and held out his arms. John and the man shuffled in an awkward dance. John was happy.

Whenever Treatch saw patients acting aggressively, he played a slow song for its calming effect. A couple of tunes later, he could go back to a faster number, such as "In the Mood."

The dance lasted a little over two hours. On the way back to his farm cottage, John couldn't calm himself down. He lay awake in bed and replayed the night in his mind, over and over. "Would it ever happen again?" he wondered as he finally fell asleep.

Bosses

In the 1950s, schiagella, a disease similar to salmonella, with symptoms of diarrhea and vomiting, was common in Lincoln. It flourished there due to the poor sanitary conditions in the day rooms. It spread easily through the patients because of the crowded living conditions. The diarrhea and vomiting that came with it only made the smells of the farm that much more memorable.

At the same time, carrying on the tradition established by "Dr. Valtairs," Lincoln only had one physician with a license that would allow him to practice on the outside. The rest of its medical staff carried "limited licenses," which allowed them to practice medicine only in state institutions.

The medical doctors at Lincoln weren't the only ones who were suspect. Psychologists weren't licensed in Illinois until the 1960s. Prior to that, practically anyone could call himself or herself a "psychologist."

But jokes about the incompetence of the Lincoln School doctors regularly made the rounds of the staff. One of the jokes recounted how two of the Lincoln School doctors were having lunch together. One doctor proudly said to the other, "I memorized all the names of the bones of the body last night, in English." His lunch partner was very impressed and said, "How did you do it?" The first doctor put down his fork, tapped his temple, and said, "I used my rectum."

Another story told about the medical staff was no joke. One of the doctors in Lincoln was as elderly as he was unqualified. He was called late one night from one of the residence cottages with the news that a patient had just died in his bed. It was very late, and the doctor didn't really want to be bothered with the news.

"Put him by a window," the irritated doctor told the attendant, "and I'll get to him in the morning."

Dr. William Fox, a surgeon and a military man with a career in the mental health field that eventually spanned forty years, was in charge of all of this. He had been superintendent at Lincoln until World War II, when he left to serve in the war. His replacement, Dr. Louis Bellinson, had such poor eyesight that he was turned down for military duty. That left him available to fill Dr. Fox's position until Fox returned from the war.

Dr. Fox was discharged from the army at Ft. Sheridan on 13 November 1945, just two weeks after John arrived in Lincoln. To Dr. Fox's credit, when he returned to Lincoln from the war, he tried to improve the notorious Sevens wards where the violently disturbed patients were kept.

In the summer of 1946, he went as far as to let the Sevens patients out of their wards on supervised walks through the grounds. The first time he tried it, half of the patients broke away, tore off their clothes, and ran away screaming, fighting, and pushing. In time, they were able to walk in couples. But they hadn't been allowed to wear shoes in the Sevens, out of fear the shoes would be used as weapons. As a result, their feet had swollen, and when they were finally allowed outside, they couldn't fit their swollen feet into their shoes. Larger shoes were ordered.

By the end of the 1940s, patients from the Sevens went marching through the Lincoln School grounds, clapping their hands as they went. They also learned to sing marching songs.

By the early 1950s, they were able to participate in recreational activities with the other patients. The appearance of the Sevens wards changed dramatically. Pictures were put on the walls for the first time. By the time the reform of the Sevens hit its two-year anniversary, it was proclaimed a ringing success.

Larry Bussard joined the staff as a social worker in 1949. He didn't get much sleep on his first night in Lincoln. The screaming and crying that went on all night was a bit of a deterrent to sound sleep.

"What was that all about?" he asked someone the next day.

He was told that the severely retarded residents—most of the twenty-eight hundred people at the main facility where he lived—usually cried out in the night. He was told he'd get used to it.

Whenever his job took him into one of the day rooms at the farm, he always stopped to light his pipe before going in. He found that the smoke from his pipe helped mask the smell of the day room. It was one of those small tricks that came with experience in Lincoln.

Bussard found himself and his fellow staff members hopelessly out-manned. In 1949, he was one of 750 employees charged with the care of 4,000 patients. But only about half of the employees were on the job at any one time. The staff members were divided into day and night shifts. Many of them were on a forty-eight-hour work week.

The job of the nonprofessional staff was to keep order and do paper-work. As a social worker, Bussard worked mostly with residents' families and the residents themselves. Writing biographies of the patients was just one of his tasks. He also tried to place those patients who could work in jobs throughout central and northern Illinois. That part of his job was not all that successful. He found a tree nursery in a small town that would hire some of the Lincoln patients and not much else.

Bussard became the chief social worker at Lincoln by 1954. He lived on the main grounds, as many of the professional staff did, for $180 a month in rent. For his $180, he received a place to live, three meals a day, and laundry and maid service.

There was a library on the grounds that the professional staff could use. Bussard had to go to the library on his second day to be fingerprinted—by the librarian, who was a working girl named Minnie. Working girls and working boys were often called on to do several different jobs, and Minnie happened to do the fingerprinting of new employees.

Minnie was a very distinguished-looking woman, Bussard thought. She was gray haired and carried herself well. At first, he thought she had to be a researcher at the library. But when he got to know her better, he was surprised to learn that she was a patient. In asking some of the staff about her, Bussard learned that Minnie's sister was also a patient. On one of his later visits to the library, Bussard remarked to Minnie, "Gee, isn't it nice that you and your sister can visit on the weekends and do things together?"

Minnie frowned and replied, "I don't see my sister."

"Oh. Why not?" he asked.

She replied, "She's a low grade."

Since most of the farm residents were severely retarded, Bussard didn't work with them much. There wasn't much hope that he would ever find jobs for them outside the fence. But he did go to the farm on other business. On his first visit there, he was appalled by what he saw. It was, he said, "one hell of a mess."

Dr. Fox brought a strict military approach with him to Lincoln. Things were to be run in an orderly, clocklike fashion, and if they weren't, someone would answer to him. If his employees reported one minute after their 8:00 A.M. starting time, he knew about it. He was almost obsessive about knowing what was going on everywhere in the school. He ran Lincoln as if it were a military base and its staff, soldiers. Employees were reprimanded for minor sins, such as walking across the grass.

Fox used the military trick of surprise inspections, which worked for a while. But then the staffers began using working boys as sentries to alert them when Dr. Fox was on his way. Eventually, the superintendent caught on to that early warning system. To get around it, he began riding in the back of the food truck as it made its rounds. When it pulled up to a building to unload lunch or dinner, he jumped out and conducted his surprise inspection on the spot.

His methods earned him the derisive nickname "Fearless Fosdick," after the by-the-book detective in Al Capp's "Li'l Abner" comic strip. Even his wife called him by that name—when he was out of earshot.

But if ever there was a place that was death to the military mind, it was the Lincoln School in the 1940s and 1950s. Trying to control it strictly was strictly a suicide mission. With its staff so badly outnumbered by the patients, to say that inmates were running the asylum was no exaggeration. As a result, there was no esprit de corps. Most of the staff members gave it all they had, but it was hopeless. Morale was in the gutter.

Dr. Fox eventually died on the job. In 1955, he bled to death from the ulcers that his tightly wound approach to the job earned him.

John walked into the cafeteria and got in line for his evening meal. He was given a metal plate, an aluminum cup, and a spoon. He put them on his tray and shuffled along in the slow-moving line.

His plate was soon filled with roast beef, mashed potatoes and gravy, and green beans. He sat at a crowded table. But before he began to eat, he noticed that he didn't have any ketchup for his beef. He got out of his chair and walked to the condiments to get ketchup. He was gone for only a few seconds, but by the time he returned, most of his food was gone.

Whenever John was distressed, he would make noise. "Aaah!" he bellowed while pointing to his near-empty plate. He looked at the plates of the people around him. It was impossible to tell who had taken his food.

He angrily walked back to the serving line and gestured for more food.

"Dummy," the food server said to him, "you've already had yours. Move along." The server shook his head no so John would understand. John walked back to his table, another lesson learned. The institutionalization of John had taken another step forward.

Some of the patients at Lincoln never gave in to the place. They fought it, sometimes physically, as with the patients who attacked staff members. The most violent patients were sometimes put in rompers but were forced to wear them backward. Wearing them in that fashion kept their arms from moving freely. It was similar to wearing a strait jacket.

Some of the patients expressed their unwillingness to give in by escaping, or attempting to escape, fifteen, twenty, or thirty times. They kept trying until they either ended up confined in the Smith Cottage jail or dead in Salt Creek. They could never accept being in Lincoln.

But some time after his escape to Beason, John gave himself up to the new world he had entered. And by doing so he found that, in some ways, this life was comfortable. The state took care of him, gave him his meals, and treated him when he was sick.

Whenever he had the opportunity to watch the dance band play, there was no other place he would rather be. When televisions were brought into the cottages in the 1960s, John found that exciting. He had Albert, a friend he could "talk" to.

John felt relatively safe in Lincoln. The routine became comfortable and comforting. The repetitive rhythm of life inside the Lincoln School had the effect of institutionalizing the Lincoln staff as well. Many of the employees lived on the grounds. They worked eight hours at the Lincoln School and then spent much of their free time there as well. New employees were told, "You'd better write down everything you know, because after you've been in here long enough, you become just like the patients." The jibe had the ring, and the sting, of truth.

The routine became like the relentless stream of water that eventually wears away rock or like the hypnotic drone of white noise. Every day was the same as the day before. A working boy would help John get on his feet in the morning at about 5:30. John went to breakfast and then to work in the day room. Even his job in the day room became more bearable. He found that the one-hundredth time he cleaned up someone's vomit was much easier than the first time. There were work breaks for lunch and cigarettes. At night, John sat with Albert, watching television or looking at pictures in magazines until the night attendant signaled them that it was time to go to bed. Once a week, Lincoln's patients watched a movie.

The patients were not allowed many personal possessions—perhaps only a comb or some items that were sent to them from home. With no family members or friends to send him anything, John had fewer personal items than most. The little he had, he carried with him in a pillowcase. He knew that if he left his things unguarded, they would be stolen.

Patients also routinely claimed certain chairs as their own. In the day rooms, they always sat in the same places. If one patient, perhaps someone new who hadn't learned the system, sat in another patient's chair, that was grounds for a fight. John learned from every fight he was ever in; from every angry, disapproving look from an attendant; and from every situation he faced in Lincoln.

Patients who were weak or too mentally disabled to defend themselves were easy marks for the predators, like Elliot, who was always watching for weaknesses. The fights in Lincoln could be vicious. John's fingers became infected when someone bit them during a fight. After another fight, he needed stitches to close a gash above his eye.

John was tormented in other ways. Knowing that John was deaf, Elliot stood in front of him and pretended to talk. That always sent John into a frenzy, and Elliot knew it.

Gradually, John learned how to fight back. The respect that he couldn't find because he was a low grade and a black man with no family and no name, he earned with his fists. His reputation as a good fighter grew. "Don't mess with John," became the byword among the Lincoln veterans.

Working boys arranged the patients in a line before every meal for the trip to the dining room. It was always a particularly volatile time. One patient might accidentally step on another's foot or might deliberately trip him, either of which would start a fight.

As the men walked down the hall for dinner one day, Elliot got behind John to step on his heel. John went down, cracking his elbow on the stone floor. He had had enough. He sprang up and went after Elliot, getting him down quickly and sitting atop him. Before the staff could step in, John had cracked Elliot's head on the floor several times, opening a cut.

After that day, the staff always put Elliot near the front of the line and John near the back, making sure they were separated by at least ten others. In the dining room, they were kept far apart as they ate.

But it wasn't only his ability to fight that helped John rise in the estimation of the staff members. He had learned another way to impress them. John noticed that patients were given better jobs if they showed that they could be helpful to the staff. He began to do small things in order to ingratiate himself and show that he could be helpful in ways other than cleaning floors. If he saw another resident becoming violent, John stepped in to help restrain him without being asked. He volunteered to take residents to the bathroom. He did the jobs that he knew the staff and the other working boys didn't want to do. John didn't want to do them any more than the others did, but he knew that this was how he could make a better life for himself in Lincoln.

John's IQ had been retested in 1950 by Dr. C. J. Bensburg, another Lincoln staff psychologist. Dr. Bensburg gave John the Hiskey IQ Test. Like the Arthur Point Scale of Performance Test John had taken in 1945, the Hiskey was created to be given to the deaf. This time, John's IQ was evaluated at thirty. Dr. Bensburg's evaluation was that John had the mind of a five-year-old, worse even than his original score from Cutts in 1945.

But the staffers knew better. They had taken their own position in the controversy over whether an IQ test was a reliable measurement of a person's intelligence. They knew very well that it was not. They had seen too many people like John—people whose IQ scores were severely low but who were able to accomplish tasks and learn things that they never should have been able to learn.

The attendants and working boys could see John's ability well before the doctors did. The Mill Tavern just outside the fence at the farm was a popular place for employees to get away and talk things over. A bunch of them were there one night, talking about different residents.

"How about John Doe?" one said. "He's come a long way, hasn't he?"

The others nodded over their beers in agreement. They took turns telling stories of how John had been helpful to them in one way or another.

"I saw him helping Jimmy to put on his clothes a few mornings ago. Maggie says he's getting to be one of her best helpers in the dorm. We might be able to use him more and more to help with things outside the day room—you know, walking the other boys around the grounds, or things like that."

"Actually," another said, "if you want to know the truth, I don't think the guy belongs in here. I think John's got a pretty good head on his shoulders."

The others knew that it was true. And the months became years.

3 Saved: Lincoln, 1955–1975

We weren't psychologists or anything, but you didn't need a master's degree to know that John had no business being in the institution.
                    —Arlie Joyner, Lincoln Developmental Center

By the mid-1950s, John's ability to help the staff and other working boys got him promoted to "class boy." That meant he was regarded as one of the higher-functioning residents and was given the responsibility of taking care of the more severely retarded. John hadn't been in a fight for some time. But only part of that could be attributed to his ability to defend himself. The fact was that the Lincoln School had become a less violent place. The reason for that was simple: chlorpromazine (Thorazine)—the psychotropic drug the psychological community would term a "chemical strait jacket."

Chlorpromazine was first shown to calm aggressive behavior in the mentally disabled in the early 1950s. It worked by inhibiting the stimulating effect that dopamine has on the brain. Its side effects were similar to the symptoms of Parkinson's disease. Patients could develop tremors in their limbs and walk with a stiff-legged gait. More serious side effects included diabetes and glaucoma.

Once its calming effect on the violently disturbed patients was established, the new drug was quickly accepted by the American psychological community. It was distributed en masse to places such as Lincoln, where it was handed out indiscriminately. The administration believed it was an answer at last to Lincoln's overcrowded, understaffed, and violent conditions. John was given daily doses of chlorpromazine as soon as it became available in the early 1960s.

Barbara Smiley's Baby

Barbara and Karl Smiley became the parents of a baby girl, Janet, in 1941. Soon after Janet was born, she was taken from her mother for some tests on her heart. Nothing else was said to Barbara or Karl about why the tests were done or what the results were. Instead, the baby was released from the hospital, and the family was happy to go home.

Three years later, Karl, a biochemist, was transferred to Peoria. It was obvious by then to both Karl and Barbara that Janet was not developing as a normal three-year-old child should. They took her to a Peoria doctor for an evaluation. The doctor quickly determined that there was a serious problem. Janet had Down syndrome. When he broke the news to Barbara and Karl, the doctor also gave them some unsolicited advice.

"If I were you," he said, "I'd put her in an institution and forget you ever had a daughter. I'm telling you that would be the best thing for her. There, she could live with others [of] her own kind. She would be much happier. And think what it would mean to your other children to have her in the family. It's going to be very hard on them to see her and live with this. Do it for them, too."

The recommendation to parents that they put their physically and mentally disabled children in an institution was fairly common in the 1940s and 1950s. Many parents simply went along with the doctor's recommendation. The Smileys did not. Instead, they kept Janet home and were determined to work with her. They were also convinced the doctor's point about Janet adversely affecting their two older children was nonsense.

Barbara worked with Janet alone until the girl was five years old and ready to register for school. But in 1946 children with Janet's level of disability were not allowed to attend a public school. So Barbara kept working with her at home. Barbara wasn't a certified teacher and had no expertise in teaching a Down syndrome child. She made it up as she went along. Things weren't going well. Barbara and Janet were both frustrated.

Barbara thought about what the doctor had said about putting Janet in an institution. She knew that her daughter was being denied her rights to a proper education. In her eyes, it was an injustice, and it made her angry. She loved Janet as much as she loved her other children and didn't understand why Janet had to be treated so much differently by society. Barbara was convinced that Janet had the potential to learn, if she only had the opportunity. Janet, Barbara thought, didn't have to be in a public school, but there should be someplace she could go for special training.

Barbara discovered that Bradley University in Peoria had created a clinic in which it trained students to be speech therapists. The university clinic was looking for clients for a summer program it had started for its students. Barbara enrolled Janet in the summer program, and two days a week, Janet attended one-hour sessions at Bradley.

In talking to each other, the parents of the children in the summer session found that they shared the same frustration and anger over the lack of help for their children. In an effort to get help, they organized a parents' association. There were about fifteen families involved. Barbara was named an officer in the association. What had begun as a mission to get help for her daughter now turned into a crusade for Barbara. She was determined to find help for all of the children in Janet's situation. She quickly became an effective and outspoken advocate for the mentally handicapped. Soon, she became president of the Illinois Association for the Mentally Retarded.

Illinois governor William Stratton was feeling uneasy in 1957. His Public Welfare Department was beginning to make noise about the conditions at the Lincoln School and at Dixon, the other state hospital for the retarded.

There had been some unfavorable articles in the newspapers about the situation. Things were heating up. He could feel that this was going to be an issue. In response, Governor Stratton did what many experienced politicians do when confronted with a sticky issue—he formed a commission to study it.

In the fall of 1957, the governor chose Barbara Smiley to chair his Commission on Mental Retardation. The makeup of its eleven members was first rate. It included state representatives Frances Dawson of Evanston and Esther Saperstein of Chicago. Other members were Jane Bull, executive director of the Commission for Handicapped Children; Dr. E. C. Cline, state supervisor of the Division of Vocational Rehabilitation; W. L. Couch, deputy director of Mental Health Services for the Department of Public Welfare; Ray Graham, director of Education of Exceptional Children in the Office of the Superintendent of Public Instruction; Dr. Samuel Kirk, director of the Institute for Research on Exceptional Children at the University of Illinois; Judge Peyton Kunce, representing the County and Probate Judges Association; Joseph Levy, associate executive director of the United Cerebral Palsy Association of Chicago; and Dr. Peter Talso, professor of medicine at Stritch School of Medicine at Loyola University in Chicago. The man appointed as the liaison between the committee and the state's Department of Public Welfare was Larry Bussard, the ex-social worker from the Lincoln School.

It quickly became apparent to the commission members that the governor didn't expect much from them. He gave them no budget and an early deadline for the completion of their work. Obviously, the governor wanted to be able to say that he was doing something about the problem without really doing something about the problem. But the commission members took their job seriously. Once they scratched the surface at Lincoln, they became very serious. What they found was just what Bussard first described when he saw the farm at Lincoln—a hell of a mess. Bussard had taken Barbara Smiley to the Lincoln School in 1951. She was revolted by what she saw there and came to the commission seven years later determined to shine a very bright light on Lincoln's dark secrets.

It wasn't the first time such a searching light had been trained on Lincoln. Even in 1946, a series of articles in the *Chicago Herald-American* had detailed the horrors of the Lincoln School. Headlined "Bare State Hospital Neglect," the articles by Richard Goodman detailed the stories of escapees' lifeless bodies fished from Salt Creek, the "jail ward" where patients who broke the rules were forced to shovel tons of coal, and the lax security that resulted in twenty-four escapes in two months. Goodman wrote about the overcrowded conditions—4,465 patients and 546 employees—and the risks a fire would pose because of the overcrowding. The institution had its own fire department. It consisted of one man who worked an eight-hour shift.

The *Chicago Tribune* followed up in 1947 with another series of articles that said Lincoln was short fifteen doctors and sixty nurses. At the time, there was only one doctor for the 1,650 patients at the farm.

The Lincoln superintendents would tell anyone who would listen about how bad conditions were. Every civic group and charitable organization to which they were invited to speak was told that the Lincoln School staff was hopelessly outnumbered and its buildings dangerously run-down. The same story was told many times in many places, but no one cared.

Now the Commission on Mental Retardation would learn the same truth. Since the commission was so poorly funded, its members sometimes paid their own expenses for travel to Lincoln and Dixon to conduct their research. They found the Lincoln School still 38 percent overcrowded with 5,381 residents between the main institution and the farm. There were 1,432 more on waiting lists for the Lincoln School and Dixon.

The commission members also learned that as far back as 1918, state officials had been told of an approaching crisis in the care of the mentally disabled, and nothing had been done. In the meantime, the problem simply grew out of proportion. The commission estimated that forty-five hundred beds would have to be added immediately at the two schools to alleviate overcrowding, and twelve hundred more would be needed by 1970. They discovered that staff shortages were severe at Lincoln and Dixon. Educational, occupational, and rehabilitation programs were nonexistent. It termed the approach used for Lincoln's residents as "herd care." Thirteen million dollars, the commissioners said, would have to be spent to modernize the buildings at Lincoln, and another $8 million, at Dixon.

In its final report, issued 22 December 1958, the commission recommended the following:

- A Division of Mental Retardation should be established to coordinate the services of the Department of Public Welfare to the state's mentally retarded, draw attention to the problems the retarded were experiencing, and carry out the recommendations of the commission.
- A full-time Study Commission on Mental Retardation should be created and, unlike the present commission, be given adequate funding and enough time to address questions the current commissioners didn't have time to investigate.
- The staff in Lincoln should be doubled.
- Six more residential facilities should be built throughout Illinois to ease the crowded conditions that currently existed.
- Encouragement and recognition should be given to public school districts that provide education to mentally retarded children.
- It should be made mandatory for public school districts to provide an education to the mentally retarded living in their district.
- Better training must be offered for teachers of the retarded.
- A full-time vocational counselor who would create programs for the retarded should be hired in Lincoln.

In a letter to Governor Stratton that was to open the commission's report, Smiley wrote, "Unless immediate steps are taken to alleviate the critical overcrowding and to provide sufficient staff and facilities to conduct adequate rehabilitation programs, the present deplorable situation will continue to depreciate."

When the report was finished, Bussard called Governor Stratton's office to inform him that it was ready. The commission members waited for a meeting to be scheduled with the governor, at which time they could formally present their report. And they continued to wait—and wait some more.

After waiting over the holidays and into January 1959, the commission members decided that Governor Stratton wanted nothing to do with their report. The Illinois General Assembly, coincidentally, was in session at the time, and they decided to take advantage of that fact.

Bussard, along with some others he enlisted to help, slipped into the state capitol early one morning before the legislators arrived. They placed a copy of the commission's report on the chair of each General Assembly member.

The lawmakers were outraged by what they read and called on the governor for action. Governor Stratton quickly took credit for creating the commission. By April, he was asking for a $150 million bond issue, which would be used for construction of new mental health facilities and remodeling of the two existing hospitals at Lincoln and Dixon.

In 1960, voters in Illinois approved the bond issue. Six million dollars was appropriated to the Lincoln School. A year later, the Department of Mental Health was created.

As the new buildings went up, Lincoln took down some of its most decrepit structures. As bad as the conditions were at the farm, which was still all male in the early 1960s, the Women's Cottage downtown was worse. It was sixty years old. Built to house 290 patients, it now had 538. There were beds in the halls, double shifts of patients to eat in the dining room, and only six shower heads in two unheated shower rooms. The wooden floors were rotting. The Women's Cottage was demolished in the flurry of activity spurred by the influx of money. When the new facilities were built, Lincoln transferred some of its residents to them. Other residents were moved out of state.

On the national level, President John F. Kennedy made more humane treatment of the mentally retarded a priority of his administration. He brought the nation's secret into the spotlight and demanded that something be done.

In 1961, President Kennedy formed a President's Committee on Mental Retardation. It found on a national level many of the same conditions that the Smiley commission had found in Illinois two years earlier. President Kennedy's committee called for new laws that would expand the mentally retarded's right to an education. Five years later, the Bureau for the Handicapped became a part of the Department of Health, Education, and Welfare.

The National Association for Retarded Children, formed in 1950, now enjoyed a boom in its membership. With it came increased political clout.

The federal government passed the Mental Retardation Facilities and Community Mental Health Centers Construction Act in 1963. It became a major source of federal funds to build new facilities for the mentally retarded. Within five years, the government would be spending $47 million for construction.

The Lincoln School used the money from the state bond issue as well as federal funds to modernize the farm's power plant, to add a laundry, to remodel the main administration building and employee housing, and to build new patient residence buildings and a mechanical shop to enable patients to learn a trade. The opening of the Illinois State Pediatric Institute resulted in sixty of Lincoln's youngest children being transferred out.

In 1963, however, Lincoln was still 38 percent overcrowded. The resident population was 5,156—and there were 1,000 still on the waiting list. There was one doctor for every 515 patients, one psychologist for every 1,031 patients.

But in the face of new attitudes toward the retarded, things were gradually changing for the better in Lincoln. Over two thousand residents, men only, were enrolled in programs to teach them industrial skills. Speech and hearing therapy was begun for the first time. Its psychology staff conducted new examinations of all the residents. New equipment and new furniture were added throughout the main facility and the farm. A new clothing center was built, which put the standard uniform at the farm—overalls and T-shirt—out. Instead of being assigned clothes on a daily basis, residents would now be allowed to choose their own clothes from a wider variety.

Thirty-nine full-time and eight part-time teachers were hired to teach special education classes at the Lincoln School. Seven consultants from the University of Illinois in Champaign and MacMurray College in Jacksonville were hired to help institute new techniques in the treatment of Lincoln's retarded. The staff psychologists created a "behavior-shaping clinic." Its purpose was to use the new techniques, and not as much chlorpromazine, to improve the behavior of the more violent residents.

For the first time at Lincoln, there were enough nurses on the staff to adequately care for its residents. The new nurses brought with them new ways of improving the health of the residents by teaching them how to take better care of themselves.

In 1965, Lincoln received a federal grant for sixty-seven thousand dollars to be used for stocking its library and setting up more training programs. Two new teachers for the deaf were hired and four more classrooms added.

Five years after the Smiley commission issued its report, the Lincoln School had taken giant strides away from its asylum mentality. Morale was rising among the staff (a big merit raise in 1965 and a first-time payroll deduction plan for insurance and savings helped) and among the residents. Overcrowding was finally being eased as the newly constructed facilities around the state began opening their doors. Lincoln residents were constantly being moved to the new places. It was inevitable that John's life would be changed by the new attitude sweeping Lincoln.

This Is the Letter *A*

Early in 1966, when he was approximately forty years old, John was enrolled in one of Lincoln's first special education classes. It had been just over twenty years since he had been found in the alley next to Saner's Tavern. If the police had been close to correct in their estimate that he was born in 1929, that meant John had spent his late teens and all of his twenties and thirties learning and living in the horrible conditions at the Lincoln farm. These were the years when his character was formed. The life experiences that shaped John into the man he had become were the experiences of the asylum—survival by guile, brute force, and an infinite capacity to absorb physical and mental punishment.

John had been given regular doses of chlorpromazine for years by the time he was enrolled in class. The drug had done its work to dull his mind. But John was gifted with a strong resolve to succeed. Given the most repugnant of jobs, he found a way to get a better one. Confined to the ugliest of places, he discovered beauty in the patients' dance band. Surrounded by hostile patients, he found a friend in Albert. Through his twenty-one years in Lincoln, he always found some way to make living worthwhile.

The first time he walked into a classroom, the experience pierced his chlorpromazine haze. He became a tireless worker, eager to learn—and capable of learning a great deal. He started by attending class two hours a day. American Sign Language was being taught so that the patients would finally have a standardized form of communication. John started by learning manual alphabet.

"John," his teacher said, "this is the letter *A*." She gently took his hand and folded his four fingers over onto his palm. She placed his thumb, straight up, against the four fingers.

"*A*," she said. "*A*."

They went on to "*B*," four fingers straight up and the thumb across the palm.

John quickly memorized the alphabet. But he could not grasp the next step, finger spelling. Despite that, his instructor told the administration that John was one of the best students in the class.

Another of his teachers submitted a written report on all of her students at the end of the year. "John's progress," she said, "was most notable in his relationships with me and other members of our class. He is much more outgoing and relates much better with others in the class than when he first started. He has made excellent progress in language and communication development and is ready to learn how to read.

"He is still somewhat withdrawn but very cooperative and well adjusted. His communication ability is still limited to gestures and the language of signs, but he has mastered the manual alphabet. We aren't even going to try math or social studies yet, but John definitely has the ability to benefit from further training."

It was becoming obvious to everyone that the initial diagnosis of severe retardation for John was a mistake.

In 1967, the first women were brought to live at the Lincoln farm, which was now being referred to as "the annex." The administration decided to house them in Annex Cottage 3, John's home. In June, to accommodate the women, the men were moved out of Cottage 3. John was moved back to Cottage 7, the one he had escaped from twenty-one years before.

Things had changed in Cottage 7. With the easing of overcrowded conditions, the residents had more space in their dorm rooms. Each bed had a footlocker, so the men didn't have to carry their belongings around in pillowcases. But Lincoln was still a rough mental institution. John couldn't toss out all of the survival skills he had learned.

Adolph Phillips took a job as a mental health technician at the Lincoln School in 1968. The position that was once called "attendant" had evolved into mental health technicians I, II, and III, each number a little higher on the state pay scale.

Adolph's job was to take care of the patients and the building they lived in. He transferred to the farm the next year, where he supervised other mental health technicians.

Being struck by patients went with the job of being mental health technician in Lincoln. But there were other aspects of the job for which no one could have been prepared.

"Adolph," an aide called, "one of the residents fell down. Can you give us a hand?"

Adolph walked into the dorm area and found that the resident, embarrassed and angry, was ready to fight. But when he saw Adolph coming to help, he went ballistic.

The resident already had cut himself somehow above his eye and had gone in for stitches. Now, he was so angry he began to pull his own stitches out.

"He doesn't even feel it," Adolph said. Blood streamed down the resident's face. He had eight stitches and fought off the staff until he had pulled every one of them out. When he pulled the last one out, he looked at his fingers and screamed, "Blood!"

Based on his behavior in class and the new-found recognition of his intelligence, John was put in charge of a group of severely retarded residents. Once he got his new job, John had to get up by himself, earlier than everyone else, to brush his teeth, comb his hair, and get dressed before it was time for the group of men in his care to wake up.

John remembered how it used to be in the day room when patients were allowed to lie on the floor and urinate on themselves. The first thing he did was make sure that his group of men knew how to ask for help to get to the bathroom. He didn't want his group to have to suffer embarrassment. Until they learned the proper sign for "bathroom," John found a way to take care of his group's bathroom visits. Arlie Joyner, a psychiatric aide at the annex, was curious about how John did it, so he observed them for a few hours.

"You know what?" Joyner told the other staff on duty, "I think John can tell time. He knows when that hand gets on the six, it's time to take one group, and when it's on the twelve, he takes the other group."

John took seriously the responsibility of supervising his group. He realized that if he did a good job with them, he would rise further in the eyes of the staff. As with the bathroom visits, he made sure his men were always treated with dignity. He had seen enough in Lincoln and wanted to make sure nobody else had to live through what he had lived through.

He approached one of the state workers on duty in the cottage. John was holding his head and stomach and making groaning sounds. He motioned for the employee to follow him. When the employee did, he discovered that a member of John's group was ill. From then on, whoever was on duty at the cottage trusted John to tell him if anything was wrong with one of his men.

"We don't have to worry about those kids John has," Joyner told the others. "He's got things under control."

Every afternoon, John led his group to the dining room for dinner. He helped the men all find chairs at the same table. After they were seated, John went to the serving line, got their food for them, and brought it to them. He would see to it that none of the other residents would be able to steal food from the men entrusted to his care. He did as much as he could for them. Albert taught John another way he could do something for his group.

"John," Albert said, using the gestures that made up their private language, "let me show you something." Carrying a pan from the kitchen where he worked, Albert led John outside and into the freshly fallen snow. "Watch," Albert told him. He bent down and scooped some of the clean snow into his pan until it was about half full. Then they walked back inside. Albert took out some milk from the refrigerator, poured the milk into the snow, and then added a large portion of sugar. John watched closely as Albert put the mixture over the heat and stirred it.

"What is this?" John asked.

"Just wait," Albert replied.

When the snow, milk, and sugar had melted, Albert poured the liquid into two bowls. He put the bowls in the freezer and told John to sit down at a table. He gave John a spoon and took one for himself. While they were waiting, John wondered what Albert was up to. When the mixture had almost refrozen, Albert took the bowls from the freezer, gave one to John, and kept one for himself.

"Eat it," Albert said as he dipped his spoon into it.

"Hey," John said to him, "this is very good."

They called it "snow cream." Albert showed John how to do it until John could do it by himself. After that, whenever it snowed, John always made snow cream for his group.

Tired of constantly having no money, John put up a shoe-shine stand on the sidewalk. He picked a heavily traveled spot. All employees were required to have shined shoes as part of their uniform, so they were always good customers for him.

One approached and motioned to John that he wanted a shine. John pulled out his rag and polish and went to work. He was a vigorous shoe shiner. By the time he finished, the employee's shoes looked almost new. John held his hand out for twenty-five cents. The employee, figuring John was too retarded to know the difference, gave him a dime.

But John knew the difference. As the man walked away, John filed the dime in his pocket and the man's face in his mind. He would never shine his shoes again.

Reform

Larry Bussard's mission to place the 1958 commission's report on the seats of Illinois legislators put him back in the minds of the Lincoln staff. Back in 1954, he had left his position as Lincoln's chief social worker. He went back to Springfield to work for the Department of Public Welfare.

From his experience in Lincoln, Bussard knew that pregnant women who were poor or unable to take care of themselves were sent by the courts to a Lincoln School hospital to have their babies. After the birth, a priest or minister was brought in to baptize the children. The children were then usually sent to foster homes. Years later, when the people born at the Lincoln School needed their birth certificates for enrollment in college or to obtain drivers' licenses, they were sometimes shocked to find "Lincoln School and State Colony" listed as their place of birth.

Learning that they had been born at a state mental institution came as an uncomfortable surprise, to say the least. Bussard knew of some cases in which these adopted children, after they became adults, found their birth mothers still living in the Lincoln School. When he had the opportunity, through his job at the Department of Public Welfare, Bussard helped ban the practice of the courts sending pregnant mothers to a state institution to have their babies.

After the 1960 bond issue passed and the state began building other, smaller regional centers for the retarded, the department assigned Bussard to be interim superintendent at the new centers in Centralia and Tinley Park. Eventually, he became superintendent of the Elizabeth Ludeman Center in Park Forest.

Back in Lincoln, after William Fox died of ulcers, Dr. Joseph Albaum became superintendent. When he retired on 1 April 1966, Dr. Louis Bellinson, who had filled in for Dr. Fox while he was in the army, came back to run the Lincoln School again.

People in Illinois were beginning to listen when they were told of how bad things were in Lincoln. In 1971, *Chicago Sun-Times* photographer Jack Dykinga won the Pulitzer Prize for a series of photos that documented life among the patients in the Lincoln and Dixon state schools. State officials knew a change had to be made.

The same year, Bussard heard that Dr. Bellinson was retiring as Lincoln's superintendent. Bussard decided he would like to be the head man at Lincoln and further its evolution from an asylum to a place that actually helped the mentally retarded. He also thought Lincoln could benefit from having someone who wasn't a doctor as its superintendent. On a personal level, Bussard believed Lincoln would be a better place than Park Forest, a Chicago suburb, for him and his wife, Connie, to raise their children. Bussard got the job, and, in 1971, twenty-two years after first going to Lincoln as a social worker, he returned.

Bussard may have been correct when he said that it was to Lincoln's advantage to have a superintendent who wasn't a doctor. But not being a medical man was going to make his job more difficult. The Lincoln School was set up to run the way a doctor thought it should run. Its hospitals, doctors, and the treatment of the residents' medical needs were priorities. Bussard, having been trained in social work, believed the priorities should be reordered to emphasize the residents' emotional and mental well-being. Big changes would have to be made.

Having seen Lincoln at its worst in the 1940s, Bussard knew how bad it could be and where its biggest problems still were. He recalled Annex Cottage 9 as being the most violent, dirty, and overcrowded place to live on the farm. Once he became superintendent, he ordered cement blocks to be brought into Cottage 9 and used to build living compartments that finally afforded the residents some semblance of privacy.

He divided the patient population among the staff so that one employee would have no more than eight residents to take care of. One staff psychologist was assigned to teach toilet training. And Smith Cottage, the building that was once used as a jail for residents, was gutted and turned into an office area.

Bussard discovered living in the Lincoln School a group of adult brothers and sisters who had been erroneously committed to Lincoln when they were children. He also found among the residents a child whose father had thought he was dead.

After his election in 1973, Illinois governor Dan Walker visited Lincoln. Bussard had tried to explain to the new governor, without success, that fixing the buildings in Lincoln was the easy part. Changing the attitudes of its staff and its residents was going to be much harder. Long-time employees had become cynics because they couldn't forget the years of overcrowded conditions that had, in effect, rendered them unable to perform their jobs. Some of the staff, Bussard told Governor Walker, had given up trying and simply settled for keeping order. Though things were changing, people changed more slowly than events.

The governor nodded politely throughout Bussard's spiel, but Bussard knew he wasn't getting through. So he changed the subject and asked the governor to take a walking tour of the Lincoln School. They arrived at the dining room at lunchtime, and the governor said he was impressed with the way it was run and how orderly the residents were as they ate.

As they left the dining room, the governor noticed an employee nearby, escorting a child with Down syndrome into the dining room. He struck up a conversation. "I've just seen a beautiful eating program," Governor

Walker said to the employee, "and you must be taking this young man in to teach him how to eat."

The employee looked at the governor and said, "No. He's a low grade. He couldn't ever learn that."

Bussard was furious and embarrassed. He apologized to the governor, and they quickly moved on. They arrived at the next building, where lunch was also being served. A kitchen employee who was dishing up food called the governor over for some unsolicited advice. People at the Lincoln School didn't often get the chance to see the governor face-to-face.

"You're not giving enough money to schools," the food server informed Governor Walker.

"Really?" the governor replied. "And what's your solution?"

"My solution," said the employee, "is to take some money away from here because these people aren't worth the money you're spending on them."

As the governor walked back to the main office, he turned to Bussard and said, "You know, Larry, when you were talking to me earlier about the attitudes here, I didn't understand what you meant. I do now."

Not long after Walker's visit, Bussard's three-year tenure as superintendent of Lincoln ended in controversy. A growing union force among the Lincoln School's employees was at odds with him over his tactics. In 1974, he resigned or was forced out, depending on which side you listened to. Bussard returned to Springfield to oversee the budget and administrative functions for ten state institutions.

In 1971, still calculating John's age from the "1929?" entered as his year of birth by the Jacksonville police, the Lincoln staff determined that John had reached the upper age limit for residents in Annex Cottage 3. He was transferred to Cottage 6. In the Lincoln renaissance of the 1960s, the cottages had been reorganized so that the severely retarded were no longer living with the mildly retarded. Cottage 6 was designated strictly for those residents who could function independently. The mental health technicians had also been reassigned so that more of them were in the cottages with the severely retarded, where they were needed the most.

The Lincoln staff decided that John had made such good progress that he could handle the responsibility of living practically unsupervised. There wasn't much supervision for the residents in Cottage 6. All of the men in 6 were working boys, as they were still called. Some traditions died very hard.

When John was moved, he was given a new job with more responsibility. He would now be in charge of many of the severely retarded men who lived in Cottage 12.

The determination among the public and legislators that Lincoln had to change meant conditions in Lincoln steadily were improving. But much damage had been done to John. He was still on chlorpromazine, along with occasional doses of haloperidol (Haldol), another antipsychotic drug that acted in much the same way as chlorpromazine. He had been on one of the drugs or the other for ten years. They had already dulled his mind. Now the drugs began to take their toll on his body.

On 17 March 1972, John became seriously ill. Staff members took him to the annex hospital, where results of his blood and urine tests showed that he had diabetes. Diabetes was one of the possible side effects of long-term exposure to chlorpromazine.

John was hospitalized for three weeks. When he was discharged from the hospital on 6 April, he was still suffering. As a result of his increased need for assistance, he was moved to Cottage 12. He once again became a resident who needed help, instead of one who was able to help the others. When he was sufficiently improved, he was put to work cutting rags in the Lincoln School's new print shop. He had been given a job as a bus-boy in one of the dining rooms but did not return to taking care of other residents.

John had fallen often in the early 1970s. At first, the staff attributed it to his general clumsiness or the joint stiffness caused by chlorpromazine. But his incidences of falling became more frequent, and the staff began to suspect that his eyesight was failing. John stopped watching television in his cottage and didn't look at pictures in magazines as much as he once did. He had no interest in the weekly movies the residents were shown. Instead, he went back to spending most of his free time staring into space or sleeping.

While leaving his busboy job with his friend, Albert, on 12 February 1973, John fell again. Albert rushed to him as John rolled on the ground in pain. John's head had hit the sidewalk hard, scraping the side of his forehead, bloodying his nose, and cutting his lip. It took four stitches to close his lip wound.

The staff was seriously concerned about John's eyes. He was issued a pair of glasses, which, in the staff's opinion, seemed to help. John was examined by Lincoln ophthalmologist Dr. Bernard Wiesbaum. The doctor diagnosed that John had glaucoma. The disease results in increased pressure inside the eye that eventually damages the optic nerve and other nerves throughout the retina. Glaucoma, like diabetes, is another possible side effect of chlorpromazine. Having diabetes also increases the chances of contracting glaucoma. And, to make matters worse, glaucoma is more frequent and more severe for African Americans.

John's loss of peripheral sight was so gradual that he may not have noticed it until the disease was advanced. He had not complained of pain or any other symptoms. Patients in Lincoln were not regularly tested for glaucoma. By the time John's symptoms were noticeable, there had already been substantial nerve damage in his eye. He probably had only tunnel vision by the time it was discovered.

The doctor prescribed eyeglasses to sharpen John's eyesight and pilocarpine eye drops to lessen the pressure inside John's eyes and relieve the strain on his optic nerve. Usually, as soon as someone gave him his drops, John went to a sink and washed them out. The staff members tried to make him understand that he shouldn't wash his face immediately after receiving the eye drops, but it did no good. The signs and gestures that they had been using weren't effective any more. It's possible he couldn't see them as clearly as he once could. It's unlikely that he realized the eye drops could help reverse the effects of glaucoma.

John's two-hour classes continued, but his performance declined. He had been taught to print "John Doe" with a marker, write the numbers 1 to 10, count objects up to ten, and sort objects according to their size, shape, and color. Now, he had lost the ability to do any of those things.

Perhaps the hardest blow was that John's ability to enjoy the dance band was greatly reduced. He could still feel the vibrations, but the sight of the shiny instruments, the musicians' movements as they played, and the gym full of people was dimming. He didn't feel confident enough to dance with anyone and usually sat at the concerts, swaying to the vibrations in his body.

In May 1973, another examination showed that John's eyesight was getting worse. The doctor doubled the strength of his eye drops and ordered him to come back in a few weeks.

But the next examination confirmed that John had severe nerve damage throughout his eyes and was going blind. "John's eyes," Dr. Wiesbaum wrote after examining John, "show no evidence of having had his pilocarpine. His pupils are large instead of being pinpoints, as they would [be] if the pilocarpine were being given. They react to light instead of being fixed as is their condition when under the influence of pilocarpine. John will go blind [and the doctor underlined that warning] if the medication is not given four times a day without fail."

The doctor ordered the strength of the eye drops doubled again, but it was already too late. The glasses seemed to help, but John wouldn't wear them unless prompted to do so. And then he lost his glasses, and the state took its time issuing him another pair. Supplying thousands of the state mental health facility residents with eyeglasses was expensive. The glasses were often lost or broken within a short time of being distributed and new ones ordered.

John was no longer able to see well enough to work as a busboy in the dining room. By the summer of 1974, a year after being diagnosed with glaucoma, he could not travel around the grounds of the Lincoln School without assistance.

John was standing by his bed when a mental health technician walked into the room. He thought John should be someplace else since everyone else was out either walking the grounds or watching television. He decided that he would ask John if he wanted to go somewhere. He gestured to him, "Would you like to come watch TV or go for a walk?" John didn't respond. The technician tried again and still got no response.

All of the staff members who worked with John had been instructed on how to communicate with him now that his eyesight was failing. They were told to face him when they spoke, keep their voices at a normal pitch, not exaggerate their lip movements, accompany their words with basic hand gestures, and rephrase their commands to him if John seemed not to understand.

But the aide approached John from the side, reached out, and tapped him on the shoulder. John had no idea the man was even there. When he felt the tap on his shoulder, he was startled. His first, unthinking reaction was to strike out. He shot out his arm, striking the technician in the mouth, drawing blood.

As soon as John realized what he'd done, he was extremely apologetic. "Uhhh," he said and shook his head. He tried to offer help to the man he'd struck.

"It's OK. I'm OK," the technician motioned to John. "Just give me a minute."

It was the first time John had been known to strike out at an employee. At the next staff meeting, the employees were told that, from now on, because of John's blindness, they were to approach him cautiously. Their first objective in getting his attention was to make sure he knew they were there. If he were startled, he would swing at them.

As John's sight narrowed and faded, the veteran employees whom John knew well had no trouble in approaching him. But John didn't trust the employees he didn't know, even when they were cautious around him. Sometimes he just took an instant dislike to them for no apparent reason. He never struck a Lincoln School employee on purpose, but when he did hit someone by accident, it was usually an employee he didn't know.

The First Farewell

The practice of using working boys to perform farm labor was on its way out as a result of the change of direction at the Lincoln School. Bussard's administration continued the movement toward putting the residents in school and teaching them independent living skills rather than preparing them for jobs outside the fence. The old rationalization that Lincoln was teaching the working boys a skill they could use to land jobs never worked. Very few had ever been hired to work on farms or anywhere else.

Farming had changed. The working boys at Lincoln once relied on horses to pull plows. But farming was becoming more mechanized. New farm machinery accomplished more work in less time than the working boys could. And putting a retarded farm worker in charge of a mammoth tractor or corn picker was a dangerous idea.

As Illinois agencies for the retarded gained more membership and more clout in the 1960s, their members realized that the Lincoln working boys were a form of slave labor for the state. If the working boys weren't going to be paid, the associations said, the system should be retired. In 1964, due in part to their lobbying efforts at the capitol in Springfield, the state decided to close the Lincoln farming operation.

Over the next year, all of the cattle and hogs on the grounds were slaughtered and sent to market. The last crops had been harvested in the fall of 1964, and the state-run farm was no more. The land was leased to private farmers.

With the massive effort to depopulate Lincoln in the 1960s, the higher-functioning residents had already been moved from the Lincoln farm. They had gone either to one of the new state-run facilities that had opened or to nursing homes or smaller group homes that had been created by community organizations for the retarded. By the mid-1970s, only a few hundred people, considered to be the most severely retarded, still lived at the farm.

In 1975, the Lincoln State School and Colony changed its name to the "Lincoln Developmental Center." The annex itself now came under scrutiny. The days of two thousand mentally disabled people living there were long over. The few hundred who remained could easily be moved elsewhere. When the new facilities for the mentally disabled were completed around the state, the Lincoln annex was no longer needed by the Department of Mental Health. The state decided instead to turn the Lincoln annex into a state prison.

Bussard, as superintendent in Lincoln, won assurances from Governor Jim Thompson that no state employees from the annex would be laid off when the transition was made. That promise secured, Bussard met with the director of the Department of Corrections to work out details of the transfer of the farm from mental hospital to prison. Bussard was directed to find other accommodations for the last five hundred farm residents and for five hundred Lincoln employees, some of whom could have jobs at the prison.

John and Albert were among the last five hundred to leave the Lincoln farm. Through thirty years of surviving in the meanest of mental institutions, they had formed a strong bond between them. Now, Albert was to be sent to the main institution in Lincoln. John would be moved to the state developmental center in Jacksonville.

In preparation for John's transfer, staff doctors reviewed his history in Lincoln. Still following the results of the 1945 IQ test, they continued to evaluate John as severely retarded. He was no longer referred to by the term "imbecile—upper division." His label had changed, but the effect was the same.

In September 1975, staff members from Jacksonville and Lincoln met to discuss John's transfer. They concentrated on setting up a training program for him at Jacksonville. Some residents at the Jacksonville Developmental Center were taught unskilled labor tasks. The jobs were therapeutic and enabled them to produce something of value, which added to their self-esteem. John was considered a good candidate for the workshop, even though he was going blind. The staffs decided that the goal for John should be his discharge from the state system into a nursing home.

The original transfer plan called for John to live in a second-floor room in Jacksonville's Coterie Center building. Both staffs agreed that, even with his blindness, John should have no trouble negotiating stairs to the second floor. But, the Jacksonville staff promised, John would be transferred to a first-floor room if he couldn't see well enough to climb the stairs.

The two staffs discussed John's diabetes and the special diet he would need. Lincoln's doctors had decided against insulin, believing his diabetes could be controlled through his diet. In Jacksonville, daily injections of insulin began.

A list of the drugs John had taken in his thirty years in Lincoln was created. It included his chlorpromazine and haloperidol, as well as a wide range of other medications, from laxatives to chloral hydrate, which was commonly known as "knockout drops." Jacksonville staffers agreed that he should remain on mood-altering drugs, at least for the time being.

John had long since shed the "No. 2" behind his name and was known in Lincoln simply as John Doe. The Jacksonville administration added "No. 24," signifying that he was the twenty-fourth unknown person to be admitted there. Having John Does become wards of the state was not an unusual event. Most of them, however, remained John Does for only a short time. In all but a few cases, their identities were eventually discovered. To remain an unknown person for as long as John had was extremely rare.

John had survived in Lincoln through six presidential terms—Truman, Eisenhower, Kennedy, Johnson, Nixon, and Ford. He had been there from the end of World War II through Korea, the Cuban missile crisis, President Kennedy's assassination, John Glenn's mini-space flight, a man walking on the moon, the Vietnam war, and the OPEC oil embargo. He had been there through thirty of the most thrilling years in American history and yet probably knew very little of it. And, for its part, history knew nothing of him.

Through those three decades when America grew from the echoes of war into a world superpower, John had grown very little. Most of what he had learned was the street savvy of a Lincoln patient who had discovered how to get ahead under the ground rules of the institution. He knew the Lincoln system and how to advance in it, but he didn't know how to read. As he left, almost thirty years to the day after he was found, he was more incapable of functioning in the world outside the Lincoln fence than he was when he arrived.

There were no fond goodbyes when John left. Instead, on 7 October 1975, a mental health technician took his hand and led him outside. He was taken to a car, climbed inside, and with that, his three decades in Lincoln simply ended.

As the state car passed the gate and headed down the highway for Jacksonville, it was the third time John had been outside the fence since he arrived. The first time was in March 1946 when he escaped to Beason. He didn't leave again until he accompanied a Lincoln staff member on an outing in 1969. And the third time he left, he left for good. And as he did, John Doe was dead. John Doe No. 24 was born again.

The Birth of Knowledge: Jacksonville, 1975–1981

I didn't get to say goodbye to him. I think, for one thing, that he left a week earlier than I thought he was leaving. But I just wasn't prepared to say goodbye. . . . I found out he died when I read it in the paper. . . . I'm sorry, I don't usually get emotional. I was just really fond of him.
—Mary Ransdell, John's teacher in Jacksonville

Reborn

Coming to Jacksonville destroyed the system of living that John had created for himself in Lincoln. John had been able to see the layout of the Lincoln farm for many years before he went blind. That gave him an advantage when he lost his sight. But, in Jacksonville, he had no such advantage. He would have to learn his way around the developmental center without the benefit of sight.

The adaptation of the Lincoln farm to a prison was going to be easy since it was virtually a prison already. If the Jacksonville Developmental Center were ever to be converted to another use, it would most easily become a college campus. Its buildings were spread over 159 tree-studded acres on the west side of the town. As the developmental center residents strolled the grounds, they could have been college students on their way to English Lit.

John's orientation at the Jacksonville Developmental Center began as soon as he was taken to his room in the Coterie Center. John walked carefully around it, using his fingers as eyes. He felt four beds along the walls and a large wooden box in the center of the room. John found the latch to the door of the big box and opened it. When he felt the hangers inside, he realized it was a closet. The closet was about six feet high, with different compartments where each man could store his clothes.

John turned to the staff member with him and made the sign for the bathroom. His room didn't have a private bathroom. Instead, residents shared a common bathroom down the hall. John was led to the bathroom. He asked to go back to his room, then back to the bathroom, then to the room and back to the bathroom again. He didn't enter the bathroom each time but stood outside and felt its door. When the attendant took his arm to guide him on the trip once more, he pushed her away. He made a high-pitched "Aeehhh, aaeeeh" and took off on his own. He found the bathroom door but on the return trip missed the door to his room. He felt the wall and was confused whether to go forward or backward. The attendant guided him gently backward to his own door. Very quickly, he had the distance from his room to the bathroom memorized.

John was given a physical examination and pronounced to be in relatively good shape. The staff believed John to be forty-six years old, based upon the original estimate that he was born in 1929. Until they had a chance to observe his psychological condition, the Jacksonville staff referred to his Lincoln records for direction. Those records still showed the "severely retarded" notation that was based on the forty-three and thirty he had scored on his IQ tests in 1945 and 1950, respectively. The notation "severely retarded" was copied into his Jacksonville records and served as the early benchmark for creating a program for him.

The Jacksonville staff met to discuss John on 10 October 1975. A doctor, two nurses, a mental health specialist, and a psychologist reviewed the Lincoln records. They noted that, in the few days he had been in Jacksonville, John had shown himself to be likable and cooperative. They affirmed their original decision to put John to work in the center's workshop. There, he would be put to work on some small assembly projects for a local industry. If he was able to learn the work, as well as take care of himself independently, the plan was to transfer him in about a year to the local Elm City Rehabilitation Center, which provided supervised living conditions for the disabled.

John liked the privacy of his room. Compared to sleeping with a hundred other men in Lincoln, it was near solitude for him. He liked the vibrations he felt at the Jacksonville center as well. He didn't quite know how to act in this new place. His streetwise Lincoln ways were useless. Though at the end of his stay in Lincoln, the overcrowded and violent conditions had eased, it was hard for John to change the way he thought and felt about his surroundings. Institutional behavior had become a part of him. Some of his behavior from Lincoln came with him when he was transferred. It would take time and patience to change that—if it could be changed.

For instance, whenever John went to the Jacksonville dining room, he

picked out the same chair in which to sit. He also became hostile whenever he sensed someone was coming too close while he was eating. He
became especially angry if someone touched, even accidentally, his tray of
food. His lack of sight only made him more paranoid about someone stealing his food.

John was also slow to adjust to the new people in his life. He needed
people around him whom he had known for a long time and could trust.
Finding them was going to take some time.

The staff at Jacksonville created a schedule for John:

- 6:00 A.M. Wake up, make the bed, brush teeth and
  wash face
- 7:00 A.M. Breakfast and medication
- 7:30 A.M. Learn to shave, comb hair, dress properly
- 8:45 A.M. Work in workshop
- 11:00 A.M. Lunch and more medication, including
  eye drops
- 1:30 P.M. Communication class for visually
  impaired
- 3:00 P.M. Free time
- 4:00 P.M. Medication
- 4:30 P.M. Dinner
- 5:30 P.M. Free time
- 6:30 P.M. Evening activity (for John, that usually consisted
  of sitting in a chair)
- 8:30 P.M. Snacks
- 9:00 P.M. Shower and dress for bed
- 10:00 P.M. Bedtime.

The daily routine gradually became comfortable. John liked knowing
what was coming next and where he was supposed to be as the day went
on. He was also getting to know the staff members, and they were getting to know him and his system of communication. But staff turnover in
Jacksonville was high, as it was at the other state developmental centers.
New employees always had the most trouble with John. As in Lincoln, he
took an instant dislike to some of the employees. He pushed the ones he
didn't like away and shouted loudly whenever he was surprised or in a bad
mood. He was reported on several occasions for "aggressive behavior."
To the staff, that was further proof that chlorpromazine or haloperidol
were required in order to control him. By this time, he had been taking
one or the other of those drugs for about fifteen years.

His poor eyesight prevented John from participating in many activities in Jacksonville. He was sent to church services until someone realized he was getting nothing out of it.

One evening, John found himself in the middle of a group singing session. A staff member played the piano and led residents as they sang. At first, no one paid much attention to John. After all, the deaf and blind aren't expected to sing. But then John felt the vibrations the sound of the piano was sending out.

The pulsing of the piano music through his body took him back to the dances in Lincoln. His memories of those dances were still strong. He couldn't see the dancers with his eyes, but they were sharp and clear in his memory.

As the singing went on, John moved toward the piano. He came closer, wedging his way between the other residents, until he was touching the piano. When he did, a smile broke across his face, and he swayed in time with the beat.

Eventually, he was enrolled in a regular group singing session. He never sang, but whenever the piano player took a break, John stepped in to pound on the keys.

A nurse approached John carefully, as she had been instructed to do with deaf and blind residents. She touched John gently on the shoulder. He turned to find out who was there. The nurse took his hand, opened it, and placed a chlorpromazine tablet on his palm. She placed a glass of water in his other hand.

John nodded that he understood, put his hand holding the pill to his mouth, and drank the water. As soon as the nurse left his room, John opened his hand and threw the pill into the waste basket. He threw his chlorpromazine away for several weeks before a custodian discovered the pills in the trash. After that, the staff members made sure he swallowed his pills before they left him.

But by August 1976, John's hostility and the occasions in which he pushed or swung his arm at people had nearly stopped. He was comfortable in his new home and was getting to know its people. He had learned to navigate the hallways and rooms. As a result, he was much less stressed. Noting his calm behavior, doctors ordered his chlorpromazine dosage gradually reduced. Even without the drugs, he was relaxed. In 1977, he was taken off the antipsychotic drugs completely for the first time since the early 1960s. But, doctors warned, if his aggressive behavior returned, the drugs would return also.

The years of medication had left John's joints permanently stiffened, resulting in a straight-legged and wooden style of walking. His glaucoma and diabetes may both have been caused by chlorpromazine, though without knowing his family's medical history, one could not possibly be sure. He had also developed arthritis, which sometimes made walking a painful experience.

Every night, Jacksonville residents gathered to watch television or to read in the residence lounge. John staked out his chair and sat in the same one every time. He memorized the path from the bathroom to his chair. Sitting in another chair would only disorient him. Having someone move his chair always sent him into a tantrum.

The staff did its best to create activities for the developmental center residents. There were regular movies, but those were meaningless to John. Most of the recreational activities and outings were a waste of time for the deaf and blind. John was left to sit alone. And then, one day, someone put a record on the phonograph.

John was sitting in his chair in the lounge when a record was put on the turntable and turned up loud. John felt it. It's a common experience for people to hear a particular song and be reminded through it of a special time in their lives. As John felt the music from the phonograph shake his bones, his mind must have wandered again to the concerts at the farm.

In his stiff-legged way, he rose from his chair and swayed back and forth. One of the nurses on duty smiled as she saw him moving to the music. She exchanged surprised glances with the other employees as they watched. And then she walked up to John, took his hands, and swayed with him. John put his arm around her waist and shuffled in a tentative version of the two-step that he had learned in Lincoln.

A grin split his face. It was probably the first time he had ever danced with a woman. The nurses and other aides in the lounge were excited that they had finally found a way to give John some enjoyment. The music didn't always work. If John was feeling ill or was in a bad mood, he would only grunt and shake his head no when someone tried to get him to dance. But when he was in the right mood, the phonograph music sent him to that place in his past where bright lights glistened from a drum set and men shuffled along a wooden gymnasium floor to the rhythm of the beat.

In the lounge late one afternoon, the residents rose to go to dinner. John was feeling disoriented that day. He was unsure of his steps and preferred to sit. Now, he could sense that something was going on around him, but he wasn't sure what it was. He rose from his chair, took a few steps, and stopped. He stood still, wondering if he should continue walking, change direction, or sit down. Arnold, another developmental center resident, saw that John was confused and took his arm. Arnold was deaf but could see.

At first, John pulled away. But Arnold gently retook John's arm and drew him toward the hall. John allowed Arnold to lead him to his usual table in the dining room. After that, the two of them walked to dinner together every day. Eventually, John let Arnold lead him around the developmental center grounds on long walks.

A friendship grew between the two men. John's blindness made it impossible for a communication system to be worked out between them. What they had instead was a silent trust. John's instinct told him that Arnold meant no harm to him. The Jacksonville staff saw that Arnold's presence calmed John and made him easier to handle. Staffers arranged to have Arnold lead John to the workshop and made sure they spent more time together.

Mother Mary

Red was a big man who enjoyed hurting people. He lived at the Jacksonville Developmental Center and attended classes with the other residents. But with Red around, none of the others learned much. Red attended class in a small room with only a table and chairs for the students and a desk and chair for the instructor, a small woman named Mary Ransdell. Red found that the classroom chairs were particularly good tools of destruction. He usually preferred throwing them on the floor but had been known to toss one through a window.

Red wasn't the only troublemaker at the developmental center or even the only troublemaker in Mary's class. One of Red's classmates, for example, had a fondness for pulling hair, including her own. But because of his size and his strength, Red was the most dangerous of all of Mary's students. He once dragged Mary down a flight of stairs, severely injuring her neck. She told her supervisors that Red didn't mean to do it, but other members of the staff at Jacksonville were just as sure that he did mean to do it.

There were six people in Mary's class. Her students were supposed to be deaf and blind, but Red was neither. He was there only because nobody else would take him. He had already gone through most of the other teachers. He attacked some of them; others he simply made miserable with his disruptions and the constant threat of violence that surrounded everything he did. Each of the instructors, in their turn, had asked that he be moved elsewhere. Now it was Mary's turn with him. The only chance she had was that Red liked Mary about as much as he was capable of liking anyone.

Mary's goal was to teach deaf-blind students to count, to go to the bathroom by themselves, and to identify their own furniture back in their living quarters. Red was the most advanced of her students at chair identification.

Mary was frustrated because she was convinced that she wasn't getting through to Red or to any of her students. On a day late in 1975, Red was in a particularly destructive and rebellious mood. He stood up during class and refused all of Mary's demands that he sit down. For what must have been the tenth time that day, he grabbed his chair and threw it hard to the floor in defiance of her. It appeared that Mary and Red had come to their inevitable showdown.

Red stood and glared at Mary, daring her to give him an excuse to hurt her. But before Mary could move, a slender, dark arm reached for the chair Red had thrown on the floor and gently picked it up. For the moment, Red's and Mary's attention was diverted.

Loud noises, such as music playing or chairs being thrown to the floor, send out vibrations. That, Mary believed, was how her new deaf and blind student, John Doe No. 24, knew that Red had thrown his chair. As John picked up the chair, Mary and Red watched him closely, but for different reasons.

From the first day John arrived in her class, Mary had an instinctive feeling regarding his abilities. Her intuition told her that he wasn't like the other students; he seemed interested in learning. Maybe it was the way he carried himself, erect and without "blindisms," such as a shaking head or rhythmic swinging of the shoulders. Whatever it was about him, her first impression was that he was special.

Red sized John up and saw something much different in him than did Mary. Red saw neither intelligence nor potential in John, only an easy victim, a slender, small, deaf, and blind man unable to defend himself. By the innocent act of picking up a chair, John had made his first friend and his first enemy in Jacksonville.

The more Mary saw of John, the more convinced she was that he was brighter than anyone thought. She believed that John, rather than being severely retarded, was capable of learning a great many things. There were others on the staff who shared her opinion. Two incidents led some of them to believe that John could see.

John was coming out of the bathroom when another resident accidentally bumped him. It was a hard enough jolt that it caused John to momentarily lose his balance. On some days, John would have let it go. But on this day he decided to do something about it. The other man kept going, and John followed him, almost running down the hallway after him, with an angry expression on his face. By the time he caught up to his target, they were both in a crowd of people. John picked the man who bumped him out of the group and went after him, punching him in the back with his fists before attendants rushed in to break it up. If John couldn't see, they wondered, how had he picked his man out of the crowd?

On another occasion, an aide came to John's room to escort him to class. When the door opened, the aide watched in surprise as John walked through the open doorway and into the hall all by himself.

News of the two events spread, and the rumor that John could see eventually reached Mary Ransdell. She thought it was preposterous. She told anyone who would listen that she believed John to be capable of many things, but she would never believe that he could see. But, her co-workers asked, how did she explain his being able to walk through the open door? How could he have picked the man who bumped into him out of a crowd of people?

"He felt the wind through the door," she said. "His senses are very keen. And the guy who ran into him, he probably smelled him, and that's how he found him. He has a keen sense of smell."

Despite her argument, some staffers still believed John could see quite well. John also had a keen sense for appraising people. He correctly sensed a friend in Mary. After class, as Mary's students lined up to walk outside, she had them hold hands in a chain. A sighted person was put at the front of the chain to lead the others safely through the grounds. But there eventually came a day when John refused to take the hand of the student next to him. Instead, he pulled his hand away and shook his head.

Mary, concerned because John wasn't cooperating, approached him and touched him on the shoulder. As soon as he felt her touch, John offered her his hand. Mary took it and joined hands with the student next to John. With Mary in the chain next to him, John walked calmly outside. After that, whenever they walked out of class, he would take no one's hand but Mary's.

By August 1976, John had shown the Jacksonville staff that he was making progress—so much that he was moved into a dorm room in a different building. As in Lincoln, some of the Jacksonville residential buildings were for higher-functioning residents who didn't need much supervision. Essayon, John's new residence, was one of them. There were fears among the staff that moving John into a new building would result in a regression as he worked to familiarize himself with another new layout. But he adapted quickly to Essayon. As soon as he had a chance to feel his way around the different rooms and hallways, he was able to travel to most places independently.

Smoking cigarettes was still one of John's favorite pleasures. He frequently held up two fingers, his sign for "cigarette," to the attendants in his new building. In turn, the staff members learned that if they gave John simple directions by gently pulling his arm one way or the other, he could understand where they wanted him to go.

The staffers at Essayon found John to be polite and cooperative. The only time they heard him make a sound was when he was disturbed by another resident. And as long as he was quiet and seemed to be enjoying himself, he was left alone.

B Is for Boyd

In 1978, two and a half years after John was transferred to Jacksonville, he was back in a Morgan County court. It had been thirty-three years since he first appeared in court and was declared "feeble-minded."

This time, the Jacksonville Developmental Center administration had asked the Circuit Court of the Seventh Judicial District to declare John legally incompetent to handle his own affairs. The fact that he could not handle his own affairs was obvious. In Lincoln, a committee was formed and a form completed that said as much. But as far as the law was concerned, John was considered legally competent until he was declared otherwise in court.

His case came before Judge Gordon Seator on 23 May. It was mainly a formality. The judge immediately issued an Order Adjudicating Incompetency and Appointing Conservator. The court appointed Russell Lovell, a public conservator, as John's guardian. Lovell would be contacted to represent John in planning meetings or before any medical treatment was given John. Lovell would have to give his consent, on John's behalf, which he always did.

A year after John was found to be legally incompetent, the state of Illinois created the Guardianship and Advocacy Commission. That commission included the Office of State Guardian, which was created to be a "guardian of last resort" for people who had no one else to look out for their interests. After its creation, the Office of State Guardian was assigned to take over John's case. Bill Ransdell, Mary's husband and a speech and hearing specialist, attempted to explain John's civil rights to him, using hand-on-hand sign language. John seemed to understand some of it, but most of the information was beyond his comprehension.

The court discharged Lovell as John's guardian on 26 September 1980 and put John under the care of the Office of State Guardian. Each of the state's guardians had hundreds of clients. As a result, it's unlikely that anyone from the office ever saw John.

Whenever John had been ill or otherwise in need of medical care in Lincoln, he was simply taken to the institution hospital or seen by institution doctors. Everything he needed in the way of health care was done for him on the grounds. His living expenses simply came out of the Lincoln School general fund.

But in Jacksonville that changed. The developmental center didn't have its own hospital and doctors, relying instead on physicians practicing in the community. Their services were not free of charge.

John was eligible for federal benefits, such as Medicaid and Supplemental Security Income, to help the developmental center pay for his care. But before he could receive those benefits, John had to be enrolled in Social Security. The process led to John being given a new name.

Before John could receive SSI benefits, he had to get a Social Security number and card. He had never needed one before. In March 1976, John Goebel, supervisor of the patient resource unit in Jacksonville, started the process. Goebel wrote a letter to the Social Security Administration Office in Springfield. In it, he detailed John's situation: "Regarding his [date of birth], we have estimated it to be the year 1929. He is unable to give any information. He is deaf-mute and partially blind. The whereabouts of his parents is unknown and place of birth is unknown. John has no income or assets of any kind and is in need of Supplemental Security Income."

But there was a catch. The Social Security Administration balked at issuing a number and card to someone with the improbable name of "John Doe." After all, that supposedly fictitious name was already on every Social Security display card the administration used in its advertising and public service displays. No, it said, there will be no card issued to a John Doe, No. 24 or No. 1 or any other number. Goebel was told that if he wanted to get a Social Security card for John, he would have to dream up another name for him.

Goebel took that news to the administrators at Jacksonville. While they didn't relish the idea of creating a name for John and changing all of his records and documentation, they did see the Social Security Administration's point. Besides, they reasoned, giving John another name would give him more of an identity. For those reasons, they directed Goebel to make up a last name, any name, to go with John Doe. The Social Security Administration said that "Doe" could be John's middle name, but not his last name. This new name, the Jacksonville administration decided, would be used only for Social Security purposes. The records would not be changed.

Goebel didn't give his unusual task much thought. He knew that he wanted to pick a name that would go well with "John" and "Doe." It would have to be something short, one syllable. But which name would it be? And how would he find it? He decided to think alphabetically. For a guide, he opened the Jacksonville telephone book and started at the beginning, skimming through its last names that began with *A*. Goebel found no short names beginning with the letter *A* that jumped out at him, so he moved on to *B*.

The first *B* name that sounded right to him was "Boyd." "John Doe Boyd. John Doe Boyd." Goebel repeated it a couple of times and liked the way it sounded. But before he settled on "Boyd," he checked a computerized list of the entire resident population of all Illinois mental health institutions. He wanted to make sure another resident didn't already have the name "John D. Boyd." No one did.

Goebel contacted Social Security with the name. It then issued number 214-82-3957 to John Doe Boyd. Only a few members of the Jacksonville staff ever knew that John had been given the name "Boyd." Instead, they continued to refer to him as "John Doe No. 24."

Mary and Bill Ransdell discovered love in a laundry room. About the time John was found in 1945, both of them were college students in Jacksonville. Bill was studying deaf education at Illinois College and working part-time at the Illinois School for the Deaf. One of his responsibilities was to do the laundry for the School for the Deaf. Mary usually came along to help him launder the clothes so that he could finish sooner, giving them some time to be together. It worked, and they were married in 1948.

After their marriage, Bill studied at Gallaudet College in Washington, which was the nation's first and most prestigious college for the deaf. He earned his master's degree in deaf administration from Gallaudet. He earned a second master's, also in deaf administration, from the University of California. He began his career by working at state schools for the deaf, usually living on the campus with Mary and their growing family.

Eventually, Bill's work became Mary's work. Bill's deaf students were some of the family's best friends. Mary had never considered working with the deaf, but she found herself fascinated by the deaf who were all around them. She eventually took the next logical step, deciding that she would become trained to help them.

While Bill was working at a school for the deaf in Delavan, Wisconsin, Mary took classes in deaf education from the University of Wisconsin in Madison. She took summer school classes from Beloit College, which offered a deaf education class by extension from the University of Wisconsin.

In the mid-1960s, Bill moved to a job in the Chicago suburb of Libertyville. Mary was asked to work in a program the Lake County Special Education District had created for the deaf-blind. There had been a major rubella outbreak in the United States in the early 1960s, resulting in thousands of babies being born deaf and blind. The Lake County program enrolled the deaf-blind children at age two and worked with them until they were old enough to attend school.

But the Ransdells soon moved again. This time, they went to Little

Rock, Arkansas, where Bill worked at another school for the deaf. It was only a matter of time. If they kept moving around enough, they would eventually find their way back to Jacksonville.

The Jacksonville Developmental Center wanted to create its first speech and hearing unit. Bill had the expertise, and he had Jacksonville roots, so the developmental center administration hired him to set up the program. When administrators hired Bill, they didn't realize that Mary was also experienced in working with the deaf and blind. When that fact was discovered, she, too, was asked to come to work at the developmental center. She agreed, but because of the growing family, she would only work mornings.

At home in the evenings, Mary and Bill often talked about John. Mary told Bill of her hunch about John's ability. He agreed with her that John was probably a victim of poor testing and preconceived notions. He encouraged her to tell someone what she thought about John. Together, they hoped that some sort of special arrangements could be found for John, since he seemed intimidated by the others in Mary's class. Mary decided that she would, very soon, ask her supervisor, Edward McEvers, for permission to teach John alone for an hour a day.

When McEvers heard her request, he told Mary that something like this would have to be discussed by the administration at a special meeting. The state discouraged one-on-one tutoring, reasoning that it was paying its therapists good money, and it would be more cost-effective for the taxpayers if the teachers taught groups of students, rather than teaching one at a time.

On the day of the meeting, Mary was well prepared. She met with six other people, including John's building director; a social worker; McEvers; and a staff psychologist, Dr. Henry Dollear.

"I have John Doe No. 24 now in my class for the deaf and blind," she began. "If you have ever seen my class, you know that it can be rough sometimes for the students to learn much. Some of them aren't interested in learning at all. But John Doe is different. I can tell by the way he acts in class that he is interested in learning. He has a hunger for it.

"John, I believe, has a lot of potential. I don't believe I've seen another like him. I think that if I could work with him on a one-on-one basis, I can do something for him. He's not going to learn anything in that class we have him in now. Let's face it, the only thing the others can learn to do is behave correctly, and some of them don't want to learn even that much. But John, I think, wants a lot more. That's why I want the chance to tutor him one-on-one.

"If you could see him in class, you would know that being with the others bothers him. When he's in his residence building, he keeps to himself. I know his records say he's severely retarded and a poor candidate for learning, but I don't believe that. I can't believe that. If you could see the way he acts in my class, you wouldn't believe it, either.

"I'm telling you, this man is not retarded. He's just never had a chance. We should give him one. I know that what I'm asking you to approve is unusual. I wouldn't even ask if I didn't think it was important. Please, give me a chance to work with him one-on-one. If it doesn't go well, I'll stop. But let me try."

There was resistance to the idea. Aside from having an instructor who was supposed to be teaching groups devoting her time to just one student, there was the possibility of legal problems. The threat of lawsuits was a constant fear among the center's staff. Caution had to be used in regulating the contact between staff and residents. Anything, no matter how innocent, could, and was, twisted and used against employees. Some had lost their jobs over false claims that they had assaulted residents. By granting Mary's request, the state could be vulnerable to a lawsuit.

Mary's career in Jacksonville had already been touched by legal problems. Most of the center's residents smoked cigarettes. They weren't allowed to carry matches or lighters, so they had to ask the staff whenever they needed a light. Normally, that wasn't a problem. But on one occasion when Mary lit a cigarette for one of her students, she used a disposable lighter with an adjustable flame. Whoever had used the lighter last had left the flame set high. When Mary lit the lighter, the fire went higher than either she or the resident expected. The resident was not injured, but he and Mary were startled.

A complaint was soon filed against Mary by the resident. In it, he claimed that she had tried to set him on fire. She was eventually cleared of the charge against her, but it was a lesson in how even the most innocent contact between staff and residents could lead to trouble.

Mary waited anxiously while her request went through channels. She had been able to persuade Dr. Dollear and her boss, McEvers, that her idea was a good one. They eventually took up the cause for her with the administration and the department back in Springfield. Permission was given for Mary to start individual tutoring with John. They would meet in the mornings, five days a week, on a trial basis. Thirty-two years after being committed to a "school" in Lincoln, John was about to begin learning for real.

Something to Call His Own

When John and Mary began working one-on-one in 1977, John had something for the first time that was his own. He didn't have to share it with a hundred other men as he did his living quarters in Lincoln. He didn't even have to share it with six others as he did when he first arrived in Mary's class. This was something just for him. He sensed that, and he responded with enthusiasm.

Mary used hand-on-hand signs to communicate with John. He was only beginning to understand that method of signing. The first step was to teach him to hold his fingers so that they were aligned properly. That made it easier for Mary to arrange them in a sign.

On the first day of class, John and Mary found the bathroom nearest to the classroom they were using. She put John's hand in hers and made the sign for bathroom. He already understood the sign, but Mary wanted him to associate it with the bathroom's location. They took a step down the hall. She grabbed one of his fingers. They took another step. She grabbed two of his fingers. Three steps, three fingers. There were fourteen steps from the classroom door to the bathroom. When she ran out of fingers on the eleventh step, she started over.

After he used the bathroom that first day, he came out with his fly open. The next time, he made the same mistake. Mary noticed it and decided it was time that John learned to remember to zip up his zipper after using the bathroom. But this particular lesson had to be delicately done. She didn't want anything to be misconstrued.

The next time John came out of the bathroom with his fly open, Mary took his hand, put it very lightly on his zipper so that her meaning would not be misunderstood and then put both her hands on his head and shook it, "No. No." He stood motionless for just a moment, processing in his mind what it was she was trying to tell him. And then he recognized it and nodded. He picked up on her meaning very quickly. When he did, they had gotten by the first uncomfortable situation that had arisen between them.

Mary's next goal was to teach John to wash his hands after using the bathroom. Part of her method of teaching John was to encourage him to use the learning tools he already possessed. Mary had discovered that one of John's tools was his powerful sense of smell. To enable him to use his sense of smell in the learning process, she brought a sweet-smelling bar of soap to class and washed John's hands with it after he'd come back from the bathroom. She put the soap on his bathroom sink where John could smell it. Before long, every time he went to the bathroom he spent four or five minutes afterward washing his hands with the perfumed soap. Mary always waited patiently for him to return. She told Bill that it didn't matter how long John stayed in the bathroom soaping his hands, as long as the lesson was learned.

Mary estimated that John knew approximately five signs when their class began. She thought that was ridiculous for a man in his midforties. She went to work on expanding his vocabulary.

There was a table and a chair in the room where they met. John, however, had no idea of the signs for either of them. Mary knew that since John didn't know the signs for such simple objects, he was going to have a harder time and would need special attention from the staff. If someone happened to move his chair in the lounge, for example, he had no way of asking a staff member where his chair had gone.

In their classroom, Mary led John to his chair and placed his hands on it. She took both his hands in hers and made the sign for "chair." Then she pushed the chair under the table. She let John pull the chair back out while she made the sign "chair" on his hands again. He turned toward her with a puzzled and frustrated look. He wondered why she kept moving the chair. Again, she put his hands on the chair and let him feel it. Then she made the sign for "chair." They repeated it many times that day, but it had no effect on John, other than to make him confused.

Mary repeated the lesson with him throughout the week. "Chair." "Chair." "Chair." "Chair." Still, there was no recognition from John.

They worked on it every day. On his bad days, John refused to even try. But Mary kept repeating the sign with her hand in his. "Chair." "Chair." "Chair." And then, one day, it clicked. When it happened, she could see it in John's face even before he knew it was there. "Yes," he nodded excitedly. He slapped his hands together and made the sign for "chair," then put his hands on the chair. He had it. After that struggle, learning "table" was relatively easy.

Mary never attempted to teach John a sign for an object unless she had it in the room with them. She brought him a variety of items—an apple, a shoe, and a glass of milk among them. Teaching John sign language was very slow work. Some of the signs Mary tried to teach him never registered with him. It often took John several weeks to learn a sign. On some days, he resisted her efforts to teach him. But those days were the exception. Normally, he was ready to learn.

John and Mary walked outside on a rainy day. Mary tilted John's face to the sky, took his hands in hers, and made the sign for "rain." Learning outside the classroom was something new for John. Since they weren't in their regular room as Mary was manipulating his hands, John wondered whether this was the same lesson or something different. As simple a thing as going outside confused him.

But they stood in the rain with their faces lifted to the sky. Mary made the sign for "rain" on John's hands over and over as they stood there getting wetter. Mary could tell when John was beginning to grasp the lesson. By now she had seen his face brighten so often with the pleasure of learning that she could practically see the thoughts as they ran through his brain. That was the way it was on the day he finally connected the "rain" sign to the wet drops hitting him in the face. Mary used the same technique to teach him "flowers," "grass," and "trees." He felt each of them as she signed its name in his hand.

After spending a year with John, Mary thought that he should learn to use a white cane to help him walk without assistance. She knew that when he was away from his room, he usually had to be led by someone or else walk gingerly down the halls with his hands in front of him as a bumper. She thought he would be happy to learn to "cane," as it was called.

But on the day Mary was going to start teaching him to use the cane, John arrived in a bad mood. He made the sign for "coffee" and shook his head no, which meant he hadn't been given his coffee that morning. Starting his day with coffee and a cigarette was important to him. He was disappointed when he didn't get them. Mary walked over to him, took his hands, and put the cane in them. She was unprepared for his reaction.

"Nanananananahhh!" John shouted. He grabbed the cane away from her and broke it in two. He was upset for a long time before Mary could calm him down. Now she was the confused one.

"Should I try it again?" she wondered. She thought that John's mood that day was part of the problem. So she brought a second cane to John and tried again. But his reaction was the same. He shook his head violently and shouted, "Nanananananahhh!" and threw the cane against the wall. He took her arm as if to say, "I will not do that. You are going to lead me when I go somewhere."

She tried the cane again, but John never accepted it. Mary knew that forcing John to use the cane would never work. She wondered whether he had either been beaten by someone with a cane in Lincoln or if he simply disliked someone who used a cane. What little she knew of the old Lincoln School was enough for her to know that John probably had a lot of misery in his past that she would never know about. The cane experiment was put aside.

John recognized most of the women on the staff in Jacksonville by feeling their earrings or, sometimes, just their earlobes. But he first knew Mary by the scent of the Shalimar perfume that she wore. When she noticed that he liked her perfume, she used perfume in the same way she used scented soap in teaching John to wash his hands.

When John arrived at class, Mary extended two of her fingers, putting one on each of John's eyes. That, she had already taught him, was the sign for "look." Then she put a bottle of perfume in his hand. She kept going back and forth from his eyes to the perfume until he realized that he was to look for a perfume bottle.

John had already familiarized himself with their classroom. Now he walked around it, feeling for the perfume and sniffing the air. He went to

Mary's desk, but her rule was that her desk was off limits to him. She took his hands, put them on her face and shook her head no.

John searched elsewhere and eventually found the bottle of perfume. The more he played the game, the better John became at finding the bottle. At that point, Mary decided to make it more of a challenge. She hid three bottles of perfume. John not only had to find a bottle, but he had to iden-tify the one with Shalimar perfume in it. When he found a bottle, he opened it and smelled it. If it wasn't Mary's perfume, he kept searching until he found it.

Whenever he came to the classroom, he came in sniffing. But Mary changed their game again. She didn't always hide a bottle of perfume. Sometimes John had to find a piece of fruit or some other object, such as a glass of milk. Class always started with the searching game. Whenever he found the object she had hidden, and he nearly always did, he smiled with pride.

Mary didn't want to end the day with their hide-and-seek game because she didn't want John to think he was getting something special because of his performance in class. She avoided anything that resembled a "re-ward-for-tricks-performed" system. John was used to being rewarded with sugarless candy or some other treat. With Mary, there were days when John learned nothing, but he was not punished for it. Whether Tuesday was a bad day or a good day didn't matter. Wednesday began with their game.

Mary was pleased when she observed John's victories, such as when he found the right perfume bottle or learned the sign for "rain." But her pleasure was shaded with sadness. She watched John progress through various stages of growth with mixed feelings. At first, she couldn't under-stand why she felt sad when she should be sharing in John's excitement at how much he was learning. She eventually realized that she was won-dering what life could have been like for John if someone would have done this for him thirty years ago.

She told her husband, Bill, that it nearly made her ill to think of how drastically John's life could have been different had Lincoln not been what it was when he arrived. She was determined to help give John a richer life, but she knew that many of his prime learning years had been thrown away, and there was only a limited amount she could do.

As frustrating as it was, she couldn't help but wonder what, if anything, they had done for John in Lincoln and why they hadn't done more. She knew nothing about the farm at the Lincoln School or that John's first job upon arriving there was cleaning human waste out of day rooms. She didn't know that they had tried to teach him sign language. She didn't know that a doctor in Jacksonville had prescribed glasses for him. The fact that she didn't know these things was due to the state's strict confidenti-ality system, which was in place for the protection of the people in its mental health system. While the privacy it gave them was crucial, the policy was often carried too far. People in different departments of the developmental center were prohibited from discussing individual cases with each other when the sharing of information would surely have been beneficial to the resident. Administrators and instructors met jointly to talk about specific cases, but too many times that information didn't trickle down to the people who were doing hands-on therapy and education.

John's classroom environment with Mary was substantially different from his life back in his residence hall. Not many of the staff members at the residence, for example, could use hand-on-hand sign language. They didn't have much of an idea of what John was doing all day when he wasn't there. As a result, most of the things he learned in class with Mary were useless to him back at his residence building. As hard as it was to teach him one set of communication tools, teaching him two systems for the two different areas of the developmental center was impossible.

One of the few times the two worlds met occurred when Mary came to John's room with an idea that she thought would help him get around more easily. She had seen how John could find his way around a strange room by using his touch. Whenever he entered a room, such as a dorm or classroom, where he was going to be spending a lot of time, he walked around it slowly, feeling to see what was there and where it was located. Once he felt the location of tables, bookshelves, desks, or beds, he could move about independently.

Mary brought to his room some wooden blocks covered with different textures. Some of the blocks were covered with sand, some with heavy-grade sandpaper, and some with satin. All of the doors at the residence hall were made of the same material and were the same size. That made it difficult for John to be sure that the door he had found was to his own room and not someone else's. To help him, Mary glued one of her wooden blocks to John's door. She showed him that when he felt that block, he knew he had found his own door. She glued another textured block to his dresser so that he would always know which one was his, even if it were to be moved. She did the same with his bed.

After she finished putting the blocks in his room, she asked a residence staff member about John's evening habits. Mary found out that John was usually in the corner of the TV room in the evenings, sitting alone and doing nothing. It seemed to her that someone should make sure that John didn't just sit there. She was told that when John had first arrived in Jacksonville, other residents teased him and stole his food and sugarless candy. After that, he preferred to stay by himself and would not participate in any of the activities they had for the residents.

A Gentle Man

Once Mary and John had been working together long enough to establish a rapport, Mary took John to her home. That soon became a regular event. Whenever they left the classroom for Mary's place, she signed to John that they were going to her house. He always nodded his head with excitement and slapped his thigh with his hand. That is the sign for "dog." In his years at the Lincoln farm, John had developed a fondness for animals. Mary's border collie was a favorite of John. She also had a Siamese cat that John liked to hold and rock in his arms. But he couldn't hold the cat very long. It made him sneeze.

Mary took notice of the gentle way in which John handled the cat. She remarked that when he held the Siamese, it was almost as if he were holding a baby. She wondered whether, somewhere in his past, he had ever held a baby. That gave her an idea.

Terry Malone was Mary's co-worker at the developmental center. His wife, also named Terry, had just given birth to a baby. Mary was good enough friends with them that she felt she could ask them for a special favor. When the baby was a few months old, Mary talked to the baby's mother.

She explained about the student she had whose name was "John Doe No. 24." Mary told Terry what she knew of John's background, which wasn't much beyond the fact that he was an unknown person and no family had ever been found.

"He is deaf and blind and has no one in the world," Mary said. "I want to try something with him, but I'm going to need your help. This man is as gentle a deaf-blind person as I have ever seen, and I wouldn't ask this if I didn't believe it was safe. I would like to have him hold your baby. I know it's asking a lot, but I promise the baby will be safe. I think it would be of great benefit to him.

"I'm trying to give him different experiences. Bill taught him 'man' and 'woman,' and we've also taught him about older children. But I want him to know what a baby is. I've been working with him one-on-one for some time, and I know him pretty well. I know we can trust him with the baby. I'd trust him to hold my own. You can stand right there next to him, and if it looks like he's not doing well, we'll take the baby back. What do you think?"

Terry agreed that it was worth a try. Terry brought her baby to Mary's room during John's class time. Mary put John into a chair and made the sign for "baby," folding her arms and swinging them in a rocking motion. She put his hands on her arms to feel what she was doing. John nodded his head to let her know that he understood that she meant "baby." While John was repeating the sign, Terry gently put her baby into his folded arms.

As soon as he felt the weight of the child, John sat up straight, and his eyes grew wide. With a touch like an experienced father's, he carefully adjusted his left arm to be sure the baby's head was supported and that his left arm took most of the baby's weight. Mary noticed that subtle motion, and it convinced her that John had held a baby before.

John smiled and softly rocked the baby in his arms. For the first time since she'd known him, Mary heard him laugh out loud with joy. The baby slept right through it.

Mary took John's right hand and guided his fingers down to the baby's toes. She moved it up the baby's body to his arms, hands and fingers. As John touched each new body part, he smiled. Sometimes he laughed too loudly. "Oh boy," Mary said as John bellowed out his laugh, "the baby's going to wake up now."

But the baby slept on. After about ten minutes, Terry carefully took the baby from John's arms. He resisted with a scowl and a guttural sound. But he let the baby go.

The next day, as soon as John reached Mary's classroom, he made the sign for "baby" so that he could hold it again. But there was no baby that day.

Instead, Mary had John sit on the floor. He seemed hesitant because he usually sat in a chair. This was not the routine he was used to. Had he not trusted Mary, he never would have let her put him on the floor. But he sat down quietly, wondering what was coming next.

Mary grabbed each of his feet and spread them apart. Then she sat opposite him and spread her feet apart so that they touched his. She had a ball in her hands, and she rolled it to him. She stood, walked to him, and helped him roll it to where she had been sitting. After doing this repeatedly, she was finally able to roll the ball to John and have him catch it and roll it back to her by himself. "Catch" quickly became one of his favorite games.

Though John could catch on easily to such exercises and some of the signs for different objects, concepts were difficult for him. When John learned "man" and "woman" from Mary's husband, Bill let him feel the faces of men and the hair of the women until John could distinguish one from the other. As John felt the man's face, Bill took his hand and added the signs for "man." He did the same for "woman" when John was ready. Afterward, John greeted Mary with a big smile on his face, made the sign for "woman," and pointed at her.

But Mary had a much harder time teaching John "friend." She used herself as the "friend" object so he would associate the feeling of having a friend with the word. But, to John, Mary was "woman," not "friend." He was confused that one object could have two names.

The value of money was also difficult to teach John. He didn't like that lesson and usually groaned when Mary told him it was time to work with coins. It was difficult for him because it combined the object—the physical money—with the concept of worth.

It took almost a year for Mary to teach John about coins. He started by feeling a penny and getting the sign for the number "one." He already knew the sign for "same," so Mary put five pennies next to a nickel. She helped John touch the five pennies, made the sign for "same," and had him touch the nickel. That is how the painstaking process of learning about the value of coins was done. It took two months for John to learn that five pennies equaled a nickel. But, over time, it got easier. He understood he could apply the same concept to coins of greater value. He slowly worked his way from the penny to the dollar.

Once he learned some of the basics about money, Mary wanted to show John how he could use what he had learned. She applied to the Jacksonville administration for permission to take John to McDonald's for lunch. Any outing off the developmental center grounds had to be approved in advance. As with her request to teach John on a one-on-one basis, there was resistance from the higher-ups to the McDonald's idea—perhaps even more resistance than for her request to tutor John. But the field trip was eventually granted. The day before she and John went to McDonald's, Mary went there alone to talk to the person who would wait on them. She wanted to prepare him for the next day when John arrived.

On that day, she put John in her car and drove off the grounds. He loved riding in an automobile so much that just being in the car would have been a thrill for him. But when they arrived at McDonald's, John smelled the food and wondered what they were doing. Mary explained, through hand-on-hand signs, that they were going to eat. She gave him a dollar and told him to ask for what he wanted and then give the dollar to the person taking his order. He nodded excitedly, and she led him inside. She stood back, with her heart pounding, and watched John approach the counter alone. What if John couldn't do it? What if he bumped into someone and reacted angrily? What if he fell and hurt himself? What if he dropped his dollar and couldn't find it? Her mind raced through every possibility of disaster.

At the counter, John made the signs she had taught him for a hamburger, french fries, and Coke. And then he held out his dollar. By doing so, he was either associating his money with something of value to him—a meal at McDonald's—or simply following Mary's instructions. She wasn't sure which it was.

Mary whispered John's order to the waiter behind the counter, who didn't understand sign language any more than he understood the biochemistry of cloning. The waiter took the dollar from John, then held John's hand while he put some change into it. John was thrilled that he had completed the transaction and received food.

As they sat at their table and ate, Mary still wasn't sure that the fact that he had exchanged money for something he wanted had gotten through to John. When John finished his meal, he made the sign for "more." John walked to the counter by himself while, this time, Mary stayed at the table, watching John closely. He made another sign for "hamburger," and the waiter, looking over John's shoulder to Mary for help after, gave it to him. When John returned to the table and started eating, Mary touched him to get his attention. "John," she signed to him, "money." He had forgotten to pay.

John suddenly sat upright with a surprised look on his face and put both his hands to his head as if to say, "Oh, am I embarrassed." Mary gave him another dollar, and he took it to the counter with a sheepish look on his face. But now Mary was sure that John understood the relationship between his money and his meal.

On the return trip to the developmental center, Mary was thinking about how much John enjoyed being in her car. She realized that a love of cars was another part of John's personality that she would be able to use as a learning tool. Mary's classroom door led directly outside. It was only a short walk from the door to the parking area. One day, before Mary and John left for another trip to the restaurant, she tried an experiment based on his enjoyment of her car.

Before they left, she let John feel her car with his hands. She put his hand on the door, opened it, then made the sign for "door." After about ten repetitions, he understood that she was showing him the door to her car. She put his hands on the hood and let him feel everything that was there. Then they worked their way back to the trunk. She stepped back and let John feel her car for as long as he wanted. When he was ready, they left for McDonald's.

After that, whenever they went somewhere in Mary's car, they did the same thing. By feeling it, John became familiar with the car's indentations, its trim, the windshield wipers, the smooth glass, and the rough grille. And then the day came when Mary decided to put that knowledge to the test. They walked outside to the parking lot, but instead of leading John to her car, Mary made him stop just as they got outside. She took his hand and made the signs "look" and "car."

He understood what she wanted. He walked to the end of the sidewalk and then around the other cars, touching each of them as he passed them. Finally, he came to Mary's car. His hands worked quickly along the sides to the front tires, then up to the car's hood. He worked his hands to the front of the hood, and, there, he felt what he was looking for, the Chrysler hood ornament on Mary's car.

He turned to Mary, smiled, and pointed to her car. He had found it and could find it every day after that, no matter how many other cars were parked in the lot.

When Shirlee Pettit was a child growing up in Jacksonville, her family lived next to the developmental center. Shirlee often rode her bicycle through the grounds. She and her family came to the center for the weekend municipal band concerts it hosted. Occasionally, a resident would wander away and end up in Shirlee's neighborhood or even on the front porch of her family's home. Through her frequent contact with developmental center residents, she learned that she didn't have to be afraid of them. Her family taught her that the residents should be treated with respect.

Her early childhood lessons were put to good use. She eventually became a psychiatric aide trainee who supervised residents in the center's workshop. That is where she met John.

Several local companies contracted with the developmental center for the unskilled labor its residents could provide. Mobil Chemical's plastics-producing plant in Jacksonville was among them. Workshop students put ties in boxes of plastic trash bags produced by the plant.

Mary brought John to the workshop to begin his orientation. He felt the room and the location of its tables and chairs. Mary put John's hand on Shirlee's arm and made the signs in John's hand for "lady, black, and pretty" and those became the signs John used to identify Shirlee. It wasn't very long before he knew her by either her smell or the feel of her face, and the signs were no longer necessary.

Shirlee brought John some trash bag ties and guided his hand to show him how to put them in the box. He nodded to her that he understood and went right to work. He still had some residual sight, enough so that when the sun rose in the sky and shone on him through a window, he called out and let Shirlee know he wanted to be moved out of the sun.

When Shirlee walked by John to see how he was doing, John called out with a high-pitched, "Eeeeee," to get her attention. She stopped and walked over to him. He was pointing to the floor, where a pile of his ties had fallen. She picked them up for him and put them back on the table. John gave her a wide grin. They had communicated for the first time, and his instinct told him Shirlee was going to be another friend.

Even though John's vocabulary of hand-on-hand signs was growing, he could not engage in a conversation with anyone. What he knew were just one- and two-sign concepts. He knew "lady," "black," and "pretty." But he could not understand, "John, this is Shirlee Pettit. She is a pretty, black woman." Putting a sentence together remained too complex a task for him. Too much time had gone by, his education had been neglected for too many years, and the years of mood-altering drugs had combined to damage his brain's ability to learn.

Shirlee, like Mary and others who had spent time with John, could see that he was not severely retarded. Shirlee thought of him as being like a young boy who never had been taught how to express himself. She was sure that he had been broken down, psychologically, by his Lincoln experience. But despite Shirlee and Mary's opinion, whenever there was a staff meeting regarding John, his records were always on the table with "IQ: forty-three" as part of the picture.

Although staff members were using terms such as "perceptive" and "learns rapidly" when discussing John, inevitably, the "severely retarded" evaluation would resurface and be accepted. No one in authority challenged that evaluation. They had John's IQ results in front of them. They knew that his mental capacity was limited. As a result, there was no longer any discussion about having John sent to the Elm City Community Center, which was the goal when he was admitted in Jacksonville. Instead, the staff members concentrated on teaching John how to communicate and to take care of himself. They were beginning to think that John, based on his progress with Mary and his recent peaceful behavior, might someday be able to live almost independently, possibly in a group home run by a community organization for the handicapped.

John was learning how to ask for what he wanted. He regularly walked down the hall from his room to the employees' break room to ask for a light for his cigarette. He knew about twenty different signs, some of which were not textbook American Sign Language but, instead, were of his own invention. It didn't matter to him as long as he could be understood. He had established a relationship with the staff members who were around him the most. He trusted them, and they were beginning to trust him.

But after he was taken off haloperidol, his mood swings returned. He could be cooperative one minute and combative the next. He was nervous in groups of people and would often strike out when anyone came too close to him. At times, he wouldn't accept help from anyone. On other days, he was congenial and eager to learn. On his good days, he clapped his hands several times to get attention and to signify that he wanted to interact with the staff and other residents.

John's hearing had been tested through the years by audiologists. It was tested again after he came to the Jacksonville Developmental Center. He showed some small reaction to the noise in his ears, enough so that the opinion was forwarded that John would benefit from a hearing aid. He was also issued new glasses. With his glasses on, John was able to copy large letters with a marker and seemed more alert and more mobile.

But Mary knew none of this. John did not wear glasses to her class. She never saw him use a hearing aid.

The Second Farewell

Red had been waiting for the right time, and now the time had come. Mary walked out of her classroom one morning and saw Red pummeling John with his fists. John was defenseless against the much bigger man and was in danger of being seriously hurt.

"Red! Red! Stop that!" Mary shouted as she ran down the hall. She thrust herself between the two of them. The big man backed off. Red still respected Mary and wouldn't strike her. Besides that, he had gotten his revenge on John. Mary took John to the developmental center infirmary for treatment of his cuts and bruises.

John continued to make progress under Mary's guidance. The staff members, noting his advancement, arranged for a new set of goals to be created for him. They designed a reinforcement system that rewarded John with points or money whenever he accomplished a task that was assigned to him. His first goal each day was to get dressed by himself, make his bed, brush his teeth, and shave by 8:30 A.M. If he could do that, with a maximum of one reminder per week, he was given a dime.

At the time the reward system was introduced, John was going through a stage in which he didn't like wearing underwear or socks. But he did like the dime. As soon as he understood that putting on his socks had something to do with getting the dime, he put on his socks. When he got out of bed, he did all of the tasks expected of him and then waited for an attendant to inspect him and give him his dime. Then he smiled and nodded a "thank you." As soon as the attendant left, John took off his socks and underwear, put them under his pillow, and put his pants back on.

Unfortunately for John, the staff members soon caught on to his trick. Their response was to buy John new shoes. If he had the new shoes, their thinking went, he would be more likely to wear his socks. John was cooperative and excited during his shoe-shopping experience and was genuinely happy to have new shoes. Instead of having them boxed, he wore them out of the store. As soon as he returned to his room at the developmental center, he took off his socks and put his new shoes back on. So much for that experiment.

As John was feeling his way along the wall of his room toward the door, he touched a table by his roommate's bed. There were several coins atop the table. The reward system had taught that coins were good things to have, so he put his roommate's coins in his pocket. He usually used the money he earned and whatever other change found its way into his pocket to buy Diet Pepsi. He liked to drink it while taking a break in Mary's class.

Another step in the effort to make John more self-sufficient was to divide his entire day into sections, with a certain task for each part of the day. If he completed each task on time, he earned points that could be used at an in-house store for residents. John accumulated points by getting out of bed at the appropriate time, washing his face and hands, or dressing appropriately (including socks and underwear). He earned more points by getting to breakfast by 7:00 A.M., returning to his room by 7:45, showing up at 8 for his medication (and not throwing it away), making his bed, shaving, combing his hair, getting to the workshop on time, staying there, taking his 4:00 P.M. medication, getting to dinner by 4:30, returning to his room, going to an evening activity, taking his 8:00 P.M. medication, taking a bath, cleaning his room, arranging his drawers or closet, and dressing himself for bed. In the morning, he was given a necklace to wear. If he still had it on at noon, he earned a nickel.

He would be given ten bonus points if any money he earned at the center or received from Social Security was deposited in a fund that was set up for him. But, rather than putting his money into his account, he preferred to either hoard it or use it for sugar-free soda, sugarless candy, or a hamburger at McDonald's with Mary.

The points system also worked in reverse. John lost points for any number of transgressions, including playing his TV or radio too loudly, talking too near others' faces, crying, screaming, stamping his feet, banging objects or doors, throwing himself on the floor, teasing others, not following instructions, exhibiting physical aggression, playing with feces or urine, destroying his own possessions, stopping up the plumbing, touching others inappropriately, destroying someone else's property, inappropriately removing clothing (socks and underwear again), masturbating indiscreetly, forcing his way in line, using objects as weapons, hurting himself, pulling the fire alarm, attempting to start a fire, running away, stealing, or engaging in sexual acts with others.

He was given a card to carry with him. His points earned as well as his demerits were recorded on the card. His biggest problems at first were stealing money, not wearing his socks and underwear, and occasionally banging his door repeatedly.

By February 1978, John's tendency to strike out at people had gotten worse. At first, he only did it when startled. But now he was doing it aggressively. Sometimes he would fight the staff members when they tried to give him a bath. He stood in his room, bellowing and banging his door for no reason. He shoved another resident down a small flight of stairs.

Mary had always patted him on the shoulder and face to show her approval. Now, he pulled away, as if in pain, whenever she touched his face. He was angry with her when she tried to get him to wash his hands in the bathroom.

He resisted when it was time to get his eye drops. The staff suspected he was having an allergic reaction to the drops, and they were changed.

John was having trouble sleeping at night. He wandered around the halls at all hours. To help him sleep, a doctor prescribed chloral hydrate, the same "knockout drops" John had been given in Lincoln. As a result of his more aggressive behavior and his mood swings, the doctors also decided to put him back on haloperidol.

A representative from the developmental center's education department wanted to update records on John's ability now that he had been working with Mary and in the workshop. Mary accompanied John to the test because he was always more cooperative when Mary was there. The test showed that John was able to follow a series of commands up to three steps. He waved "hello" and "goodbye." He knew the signs for most articles of clothing, eating utensils, and some common household objects. He could button, snap, and zip items. She found him to be primarily right-handed. He printed "John" for her and could copy a few letters if the type were large enough. John identified for her each of the letters of the alphabet and the words "want," "run," "one," "ball," and "food." He also identified a penny, nickel, dime, and quarter.

Those things he could accomplish, of course, he owed to Mary's instruction and his own determination. They had worked together for more than a year. In that time, John had made more progress than he had in thirty years in Lincoln. It was obvious to Mary that her original hunch about John's ability was correct.

Though Mary had originally been able to convince the developmental center administration that she should tutor John one-on-one, the issue of money kept coming up. It still rankled some people that she was spending an hour a day with just one person. Mary was told that she would have to stop. She would go back to teaching groups of residents only, and John would become more involved in the center's other programs for the deaf and blind.

Mary was extremely unhappy about the decision, but she knew that there was nothing she could do about it. John would also be spending more time in the workshop. Mary was given a new classroom just off the workshop area, so she would be near John if he or the staff needed her.

About two years after they began, her daily sessions with John stopped.

They still saw each other nearly every day, but the transition away from their daily sessions was hard on them both. Mary was enraged the day she drove onto the grounds and saw John walking alone down the middle of the road. One of the other staff members was supposed to be taking him for a supervised walk. Instead, as Mary drove closer, she saw the staffer standing on a sidewalk while John walked out into the street alone.

Mary stopped her car and asked the attendant, "Why are you letting him do this?"

"Well," he answered her, "I think this is sort of like Pavlov's theory with the dogs. You have to train these people the same way you train a dog. If he walks out there and happens to get hit by a car, he'll know to stay out of the street from then on."

Outraged, Mary helped John back to the sidewalk, got back into her car, and went directly to the administrative office to report what she had seen. After that, she was worried about what would happen to John. But she had to let him go.

In her twenty years of working with the deaf and blind, Mary never became as close to another student as she did to John. After their sessions ended, she tried to check on John's progress but couldn't learn much about him because of the state's confidentiality rules.

For John's part, if he ever experienced the sensation of love, it was when he knew Mary. He expressed his feelings for her in many ways—through his eagerness to go to her class, by accomplishing whatever she asked of him, by stalking the halls and muttering angrily on the days when they weren't together, by refusing to walk outside with anyone but her, and by wanting to wear the same Shalimar perfume Mary wore. He was jealous if he sensed that Mary was giving other residents any attention. His affection for her, complete with its immature jealousy and demands for her full attention, was similar to what a child feels for its mother. Mary had nurtured John. She led him through his first steps toward the knowledge of the world around him.

First, Albert had gone from John's life, and now it was Mary. Unfortunately, there would be many more who followed the same path, abruptly entering and leaving John's life.

How Far John Will Go

In May 1974, on his first day of work at the Lincoln Developmental Center, Willie Glaze wore a white suit. That was a rookie mistake.

He was being given the obligatory "first day" tour of the grounds of Lincoln when he saw a patient stop by a tree. Willie hadn't had much experience in a large facility for the mentally handicapped, and he wanted to prove that he was not afraid of the patients. He walked over to the man by the tree, intending to say hello. What he had not seen was that the man had just defecated, which was why he had walked behind the tree in the first place.

As Willie approached the man to say hello, the man leaned toward him and smeared feces down the arm of Willie's white suit. Willie was stunned and embarrassed. The developmental center paid to have the suit cleaned, but Willie never wore it again. He had learned lesson number one at Lincoln: approach the residents with caution, especially if they are standing behind a tree.

Willie was a student at Rockhurst, a Jesuit college in Kansas City, when he first developed an interest in helping the deaf. Through the Jesuits, he met several nuns who worked with the disabled in Kansas City's inner city. At the time, he was a communications major and had every intention of becoming a school teacher. But that changed when he volunteered to work with the sisters.

They taught Willie the fundamentals of working with people who were deaf. He explored the educational options in that field and decided to transfer to Marquette University in Milwaukee, where he eventually earned his master's degree in speech language pathology. At Marquette, he had his first experience with the deaf-blind.

On breaks from school, he drove south to see his family in New Orleans. He took Interstate 55, which passed right by the Lincoln Developmental Center. Whenever he saw the signs near the exits for the developmental center, he wondered what it was. On that first day of working there, he found out.

Willie started as a speech language pathologist at Lincoln and was assigned to work at both the main institution and the annex. In 1975, Willie received a promotion and moved to the Jacksonville Developmental Center to become a hearing and speech specialist. That's where he first met John Doe No. 24.

Not long after John's breakfast each day, a Jacksonville staff member walked into his room. Careful not to startle him, she reached out to touch his shoulder. He turned in her direction, and she took his hand. She placed her hand on his and signed "school." She took his arm and led him out of his room and down the hall.

As they went, they picked up more people until there was about a ten-person train walking down the hall—five residents and five staff members. John dragged his hand lightly along the wall, a method of navigation called "trailing." Other blind residents preferred to feel the stainless steel bars that had been installed along the wall. John wouldn't touch them. He didn't like the feel of the cold metal bar. Whenever he came to a recessed door, where there was no wall for him to touch, the staff member with him tapped him on the hand. That was his signal to walk past the doorway.

The "train" eventually arrived at Jacksonville's deaf-blind training area. Harriet Conner, John's instructor in the program, became his main teacher after he no longer attended Mary's class.

Once they reached the classroom, each resident in the deaf-blind program was taken to a different area. John was led to a small wooden flight of stairs. There were two steps up, then a plateau and two more steps down. A staff member gently put John's hands on the railings and let him lean forward. He felt the first step tentatively with his right foot. When he found the top, he rose and put both feet on the step. He raised his right foot again and found the next step. Up again. Then, on the plateau, he raised his foot but found no step. "Uhh? Uhh?" he said with a cock of his head.

The staff member slid John's foot forward and off the plateau. John, still holding the rails, felt air with his foot. It slowly went down until he felt the solidity of the first step. He put his weight on the foot, and it held. He stepped down—and down to the next step—and down to the floor.

He was led to a group of boxes on the floor. There were six small boxes on the right and seven small boxes on the left. With John's hands gripping support railings, the aide picked up John's right foot and placed it in the first box. Then his left foot was placed in a box. Each time, the aide picked up John's foot and placed it in the next box until John had walked through them all.

John was taught how to shave his face, comb his hair, and fold his clothes. He felt different textures, he smelled a variety of odors, he learned his left from his right, and he learned more basic signs for food items.

Every weekday was the same. Just as it had been in Lincoln, the routine in Jacksonville was a source of comfort and security to John that helped ease the loss of Mary.

After dinner, John went to his room. He didn't participate in many activities, rarely sat with the others in the lounge, and preferred instead to slip off to his room and sleep. If he had a chance during the day, he would sneak into his room for a nap. The staff members kept trying to encourage him to participate in events, but he preferred to be alone. When they insisted that he come to the TV room, he sat alone in the same chair he always sat in. His dancing days seemed to be over for good.

John made progress in the deaf-blind program. He had learned the hand-on-hand signs for "work," "time to go," and "stand up." Harriet Conner said John could identify a brush, comb, shoe, sock, shirt, pants, bed, pillow, chair, door, window, and clothes hanger. When given signed instructions, he could put items into a box and close the lid. He worked on stringing together blocks of different shapes and putting plastic circle and square puzzles together. He was taught to write "John" on a blackboard. Harriet was teaching him how to tell time by feeling the hands of a clock.

The administration revived the idea of mainstreaming John into the community, rather than transferring him to another facility, such as a nursing home or care center. They set a new deadline of May 1980 for discharging him from Jacksonville.

Ruth Brown of the Jacksonville Developmental Center was assigned to work in the deaf-blind program at Jacksonville. Before she started, she was sent for training to the Helen Keller National Center for Deaf-Blind Youths and Adults (HKNC) in New York. It was the only place in the country devoted exclusively to people who were both deaf and blind.

The Helen Keller Center was on prime Long Island real estate in the town of Sands Point, next to Port Washington, a city once found to have the highest per capita income in the United States. The center was built on a twenty-five-acre point jutting into the south side of Long Island Sound. The navy once used the site as a training station.

An act of Congress established the Helen Keller Center in 1967. It evolved from the Industrial Home for the Blind (IHB) in Brooklyn, a pioneer in the education and training of the deaf-blind. The IHB discovered that there were more deaf-blind people in the country than anyone had imagined. It also found that those people were being neglected. In the spring of 1967, Dr. Peter Salmon, director of the IHB, testified before Congress concerning the need to establish a national center for the deaf-blind. The legislators agreed.

The center opened in June 1969 in a warehouse in New Hyde Park, New York. Its eighteen staff members and residents outgrew the warehouse as soon as it opened. The search began for a new location. That's when the government offered its twenty-five acres of naval training center on Sands Point. Construction of a new center began in 1971. It opened in 1976.

No resident of the Jacksonville Developmental Center had ever gone to the Helen Keller Center for training. Candidates had to show that they had the intellectual capacity to learn under the more rigorous atmosphere at Helen Keller. Ruth Brown was convinced that if any of them could qualify, it would be John.

John was likely in his early fifties when the idea of sending him to New York surfaced. Ruth thought that John seemed ready to make the leap to the more complicated tasks that he would be taught in New York. To prove it, she put him through a series of tests. During one of them, she sat at a table with him and spread out a comb, a shoe, and a spoon before him.

She picked up the comb and signed in his hand, "comb." She put the comb in his hand and let him feel it. He ran his fingers along its teeth. Then she took it from him and put it back on the table.

"This is a shoe," she signed to him, and he ran his hands over the shoe. She did the same thing with the spoon. Then she signed in his hand, "Comb. Give me comb." John ran his hands around the table, located the comb, and gave it to Ruth.

"Good," she signed to him. He did the same with the other objects. He passed the test. New York seemed more of a possibility than ever.

On 30 November 1979, Linda Gladstone from the Helen Keller Center arrived in Jacksonville to evaluate John. After seeing what he could do, and after talking to the staff at the developmental center, she arranged for John to be sent to the Chicago Lighthouse for the Blind, the Midwest screening center for potential Helen Keller clients.

On 17 January 1980, John left Jacksonville to be examined in Chicago. Harriet Conner rode with John in the back of a state van as it traveled up Interstate 55 for the four-hour trip. There wasn't much heat in the back of the van. John complained of the cold and was moved to the front, closer to the heater.

At the Chicago Lighthouse, John felt his way around the examining room, using his sense of touch to acclimate himself. When he felt comfortable, the examination began. Dale Berger-Daar, coordinator of the Lighthouse's deaf-blind program, and Dr. Arthur Neyhus, a psychological consultant from the University of Illinois, tested John. Gladstone, the Helen Keller Center representative, was present to observe the tests.

"John," Berger-Daar said loudly, his face very near John's, "can you make this sound—el, el, el? Can you do that?" And John said, clearly enough to be understood, "El."

"Very good," Berger-Daar said, loudly again. "Now try this one—buh, buh." And John said, "Buh."

"Alright, John, let's try this." He brought a stereo speaker next to John's left ear and turned on the music. John showed no reaction. He put the speaker next to John's right ear, and John cocked his head toward the speaker as if straining to hear.

Peg boards were placed in front of John. Berger-Daar signed to John that he was to place the pegs in their holes. John accomplished it without any difficulty, but he had trouble putting a puzzle together. Though he may not have remembered, it was similar to the puzzles that John had seen when Richard Cutts had given him his IQ test back in 1945. He was able to fit some of the shapes into their proper places but worked very slowly. Berger-Daar speculated that John's poor finger dexterity might be due to the years of chlorpromazine and from the haloperidol that John was still taking.

An examiner put one block atop another block. He showed John the small stack and signed for him to build a stack of his own, which he did.

He put three pennies in front of John and guided his fingers to them. Then he had John pick out some blocks. He signed to him that he wanted him to cover the pennies with the blocks. John did it.

They sat on the floor and rolled a ball back and forth between the two of them. It was the old game John had played with Mary Ransdell, and he could do it easily. But then a third person was added, changing the pattern. John seemed confused at first but eventually learned the right sequence for rolling the ball. Then a fourth and a fifth person were added to the circle. Each time, John was able to determine where the ball would be coming from and where he was to roll it.

Berger-Daar was impressed with John's ability and the way John cooperated with the Lighthouse staff members, even though they were unfamiliar to him, as was the place in which he was tested. "I think he'd be a good candidate for the Helen Keller Center," he later wrote to the administration at the Jacksonville Developmental Center. "The kind of intensive training he would receive there would be a benefit to him."

In June 1980, Gladstone wrote to Olga Jackson, a counselor at Jacksonville, saying that the staff at the Helen Keller Center agreed with Berger-Daar that John would be a good candidate. "I was very impressed," she wrote, "with the ease and manner in which John was able to perform the tasks [in Chicago]. I believe that the intensive training he would receive at HKNC would best develop his skills, both personally and vocationally, and allow him the opportunity to become a useful member of his home community." She enclosed an application form for John.

Jackson replied that she would like to have John come to the Helen Keller Center, but it wasn't simply a matter of finding him to be a good candidate and then putting him on a plane for New York. First, a plan had to be created for John's life after he came back from Helen Keller. Until that was done, he wasn't going anywhere. Second, the administration at Jacksonville was concerned about payment for John's stay in New York. He only received twenty-five dollars a month from Social Security Supplemental Security Income. His daily "pay" of twenty cents for following the rules and another twenty cents for working in the workshop wasn't going to help.

Lowell Sanborn, a counselor for the blind from the Illinois Department of Rehabilitation Services, was asked to intervene on John's behalf. After reviewing John's situation, Sanborn said there was an excellent chance that the state of Illinois could help find the money to pay for John's stay at the Helen Keller Center. It seemed certain that John was going to New York.

A Suit, a Tie, and an Airplane

John had been in Jacksonville for five years. He'd been on and off haloperidol and chlorpromazine most of that time as he yo-yoed between being physically aggressive and docile. His dosage of haloperidol had been reduced again late in 1980. The goal was to have him taken off it completely before he left for New York.

His eyesight had deteriorated to the point where he no longer noticed bright sunlight. He was receiving two kinds of eye drops and was checked by an ophthalmologist every three months. But he was completely sightless.

Most of the Jacksonville staff still regarded him as severely mentally retarded. His IQ, as far as they were concerned, was still forty-three. John was suffering the effects of thirty-five years of what the experts termed "psychosocial environmental deprivation" in state institutions.

In 1979, the staff noticed that the right side of John's face seemed to be drooping. A doctor who examined him believed John had suffered a mild stroke. He recommended no further treatment for the condition, but he said John should be monitored closely.

According to tests administered to John in 1980, he had regressed over the past year, very likely due to the effects of the stroke. His socialization skills had declined. His eyesight had declined. And his ability to communicate had also been reduced. At one time, he could use seventy signs, but that number was going down.

He had been taken off insulin in 1979 in favor of controlling his diabetes through his diet. Instead, his diabetes had gone out of control for months before it was caught. Technicians had reported that John preferred to lie in bed and had become less independent. He had become much harder for them to handle. A subsequent physical exam showed that his blood sugar was dangerously high, and it was most likely having an effect on his behavior. Daily insulin injections were resumed.

By 1980, John's training consisted of daily sessions in the deaf-blind program and the workshop. Under Harriet Conner's direction in the deaf-blind area, he was stringing together small beads, climbing steps, walking a balance beam, putting puzzles together, and riding an exercise bike. In the workshop, one of his jobs was putting screws into envelopes. Sometimes, he put four or five screws into an envelope that should only have three. In the past, he was able to recognize that mistake and correct it. But recently, he no longer could because his sense of touch had degenerated. Doctors blamed that on the effect of regular insulin injections.

John's therapists were putting more emphasis on his ability to interact with people. He usually smiled and turned toward whoever was communicating with him. His range of signs and gestures had increased, until his regression of the past year. The therapists wanted John evaluated again for a hearing aid, even though their tests showed that his hearing loss was so profound that a hearing aid probably wouldn't do much good.

In late 1980, John was five feet, six inches tall and weighed 152 pounds, which, it was noted, was about 10 to 15 pounds overweight. He had gained 12 pounds in the last year.

John could brush his own teeth and dress himself, identifying all of his clothing independently. He could tie his own shoes. But his ability to toilet himself had also deteriorated in the past few months. That was attributed to the fact that he was attending a communication skills class in a new area. Since it was new to John, it was assumed that he would regress while he adjusted to the new surroundings. John's orientation and memory for locations were good enough for him to get by only when he was in a familiar place.

Because of his lively response to music, John had been enrolled in a rhythm band class. John had also been sent to a religion class to enrich his spiritual growth. A minister reported, however, that John did not respond to any of his attempts to communicate with him.

In his five years in Jacksonville, John found a few things that gave him joy. One was Mary. The other was the piano. And, like The Who's "deaf, dumb, and blind kid," John played a pinball machine.

In early 1981, Lowell Sanborn contacted the developmental center administrators to tell them adequate funding for John's assignment to New York had been found. The state's Department of Rehabilitation Services and Social Security Supplemental Income would foot the bill. John would be leaving for New York in April.

In anticipation of John's discharge, his dosage of haloperidol was eliminated. But the staff was told to watch John closely. If he became physically aggressive again, he would be put back on haloperidol. Weeks went by, and there were no incidents of violence from John.

Willie Glaze and other staff members tried to prepare John for his upcoming trip. One of the first goals was teaching John the sign for "airplane." Once that was done, they put him in a swing and pushed him in an attempt to simulate the motion of an airplane taking off—all the while making the sign for "airplane" in John's hand. After that, they put his hands on a table while a couple of them pounded the table with their fists. They played music and put the speaker face down on the table so that he could feel the vibrations as if he were experiencing a plane's engines revving up. John's response was to tap his fingers to the beat of the vibrations he felt.

Willie had doubts that any of their efforts were leading John to connect what they were doing to the fact that he was going to be riding in an airplane. Sometimes, as they were pounding on the table or pushing John in the swing, John looked at them and laughed as if to say, "You are all very silly. Of course I know what an airplane is."

The general "uniform" for Jacksonville residents was strictly practical—they wore trousers with elastic waists and no belts, for example. The staff decided that, for his trip to New York, John should wear something less institutional. The staff included clothing aides, people whose job was to launder and distribute clothing. Two of those aides were given the job of taking John downtown in Jacksonville to buy him some new clothes. They picked out for him a dark suit, white shirt, and dark tie. They topped it with a hat with a red feather and a London Fog overcoat.

Early on 28 April 1981, John and Willie left for New York. John walked out the door wearing his new suit, the hat with the red feather, and his new coat slung over one arm. He looked a bit like a banker.

The nurses and other staff members hugged John and cried as he left. The men shook John's hand, patted him on the back, and wished him luck.

At 6:45 A.M., John and Willie got into a state-issue station wagon with large Illinois Department of Mental Health decals on its sides and set off for Lambert Field in St. Louis. John carried $16.70 in his pocket and an SSI check for $20.00.

Mary Ransdell doesn't remember that day. It was just another day at the developmental center for her. She did not know that it was the day John was leaving. The two of them never had a chance to say goodbye to each other.

It was windy in St. Louis. When John and Willie arrived at their gate at the airport, they found it had no jetway. They had to walk onto the tarmac and up a flight of steps in order to board. Willie put John's foot on the first step up to the plane and made the sign for "step" into John's hand. John knew how to walk up steps, but this was going to feel different for him, especially with the strong wind blowing. But once he got past the first couple of steps, he walked the rest of the way without much help from Willie.

John, as luck would have it, got the window seat. Willie put his own seat belt on and let John feel how it was put together. John nodded. Then Willie clicked John's belt and pulled it—but not so tight that John felt too restrained. Willie was nervous enough, wondering how John would react to the flight, without having John struggle against a too-tight seat belt. As the plane prepared for takeoff, Willie wondered how he could let John know what was going to happen. He took John's hand, put it on his own, and tried to simulate the action of the plane leaving the ground. He made a swooshing motion with their two hands and hoped that would somehow register with John. But when the plane left the ground, John was strictly a white-knuckle flyer. The force of takeoff pushed John back into his seat. His eyes grew wide, and he hung onto the armrest tightly.

After the plane leveled off and the passengers, including John, relaxed, it was time for lunch. As the flight attendant put John's plate before him,

John felt around it to find out where everything was located. He felt his utensils and found, to his chagrin, that they were wrapped in plastic. This, too, was something new, and it confused John. Willie took John's utensils and began to tear open the plastic, but John slapped him on the hand, took the plastic bag, bit it with his teeth, and opened it on his own.

Willie reached over to cut John's meat for him. But John slapped his hand away again, picked up the knife and fork, and cut it himself. Willie had never known John to do that. John had shouted and made enough of a commotion when he slapped Willie's hand that the other passengers were staring at them, wondering what was going on. Willie, embarrassed, leaned over and whispered in John's ear, even though he knew that John couldn't hear him. "Oh, I see," Willie whispered, "I see how you are now." John, probably feeling Willie's breath on his cheek smiled. To the other passengers, it appeared as if they were having an enjoyable conversation.

After that, whenever John needed something, he tapped Willie on the shoulder. Otherwise, Willie thought it was a good idea to leave him alone.

They landed at LaGuardia Airport in New York City, where Helen Keller staff members were waiting for them. After the introductions, they boarded a van and started for the center on Long Island. As soon as they met John, members of the staff began using hand-on-hand sign language with him. They had already been told which signs John understood. Unlike the staff in Jacksonville, where only a few knew hand-on-hand, everyone at Helen Keller who would be working with John would be using sign language with him.

The plan was for Willie to stay with John until John had comfortably made the transition between Jacksonville and New York. Each day, Willie would take a smaller role in John's care, and the Helen Keller staff would take a larger role. Willie was prepared to stay for weeks while John adjusted. But John adapted to his new surroundings so easily that Willie left him in New York after only a few days.

"When John got to Helen Keller," Willie reported to the Jacksonville staff when he returned, "they fell in love with him."

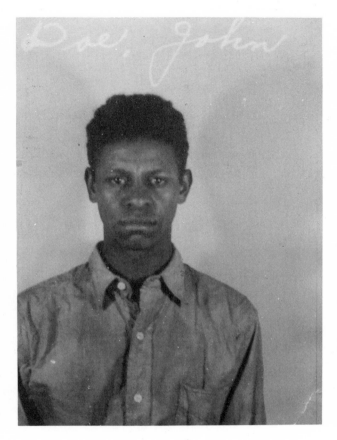

John Doe No. 24, 1945. The handwritten words "John Doe" appear just above his head. He would not be photographed again for over thirty years. Courtesy Illinois Department of Human Services.

south door in Hall way, south of the office, the
party or parties had taken a large Seth Thomas
8-Day Clock, from Wall in Storage Room down
hall way from Business office between 9:ᵒᵒ P.M.
Oct. 11 & 7:ᵒᵒ A.M. Oct. 12ᵗʰ blood was left on
window. Sgt Court made Investigation.

8:³⁰
a.m.

Officer Nunes reported that Mr Woods living
next door south of his home, 838 N. Church
had passed away, & that Dr. Wolfe was called.
Coroner Deputy Timmons was notified by this
Department & said he would take charge.
Coroner Young could not be located

9:45
a.m.

Officer Carter & Wilson from bank to Factory
with Mrs Benson at 9:³⁰ a.m & Smith at 9:45 a.m.

Norbury Sanatorium So. Diamond St. reports
Leland Spalzberth 36, 5'10, 162, Brown Coat
Brown Trousers & Hat. Escaped. Officer Wiant &
Wilson were on call. (Man not located.)

10:³⁰
a.m.

Officer Wiant & Wilson took colored boy to
County Jail, Sheriff will see that he is taken
care of.

11:²⁰
a.m.

State notified this Dept. that the colored boy
has not Escaped Dixon State Hospital or
Lincoln State School. Ref. message 6609
was picked up by East St. Louis Police Dept.
Oct. 8ᵗʰ & Green Co. Sheriff Oct. 10 ᵗʰ and
released by both Depts.

11:³⁰
a.m.

Chief & Carter to West State & church St, to check
a car. Ind. Lic. 263-744 Ford (name Gladhart
in car) Car at Suksman's Garage. Released
owner Maryann Gladhart Winchester Rd.

1:⁴⁵
p.m.

Chief Carter & Wilson to So. Diamond to check on a
man with chickens In Sack. reported by Deputy Jones
No one located

Entries from the Jacksonville Police Department log, October
1945, concerning a "colored boy" taken into custody. The
"colored boy" was John.

STATE OF ILLINOIS,   } ss.   In the County Court of said County.
County of......**MORGAN**..................}

In the Matter of......**JOHN DOE**.., an Alleged Feeble-Minded Person.

To the Honorable Judge......**Paul Fenstermaker**.................................County Judge of said County:

The undersigned, a Commission heretofore appointed by an order of this Court to make a personal examination of the said

......**John Doe**..................................., alleged to be feeble-minded, would respectfully report

that in pursuance of their appointment and the order aforesaid, they did, on the......**29th**......day of......**October**......

A. D. 19**45**., make a personal examination of the said......**John Doe**...

and as a result of their inquiries they report that they find the said ...**John Doe**....................................

....

....

....

....

....

....

....

from which they conclude that ...he is......**feeble-minded**......................................and that it is for the interest of said

person and the People of the State of Illinois that said person be committed to the State Institution for feeble-minded persons.

Your Commission would further report that we have answered such interrogatories as have been furnished us, propounded

by the Department of Public Welfare, as seem to apply to this particular case, and verified the same by an affidavit to the best of

our knowledge and belief, which said interrogatories are hereto attached and marked "Exhibit A" and made a part of this report.

......................................*[signature]*..................M. D.⎫
......................................*[signature]*..................M. D.⎬ Commission.
....Ph. D.⎭

"Exhibit A"—Interrogatories and Answers.

STATE OF ILLINOIS,   } ss.   In the County Court of said County.
County of......**MORGAN**..................}

In the Matter of......**JOHN DOE**...an Alleged Feeble-Minded Person.

Name (in full)..

Residence.., County..

Age..................Native of...Duration of residence in the U. S....................

If less than two years in this country, state exact date of arrival and, if possible, the ship on which ...he was brought to this

country...

Duration of residence in Illinois..

Place from which ...he came to this State..

Is h........ pecuniary or financial condition such that ...he can reimburse the State, in whole or in part, for the cost of h.........

support and treatment?..

Does the individual, husband or wife, either parent, or any child of the individual own real estate in Illinois? If so, state

particulars..

Has the individual, husband or wife, either parent, or any child of the individual, paid taxes in this State within the last

three years?.............. If so, who, when and in what city or town?...

Has ...he a conservator or guardian, relatives or friends who are liable, or may be willing to assume, in whole or in part, the

costs of h........ support and treatment?......................... Correspondent's name and address..............................

....

The court finds John "feeble-minded."

(To be executed in duplicate, one to be kept by the Superintendent of Lincoln State School and Colony, and the other to be returned to the Clerk of the County Court.)

STATE OF ILLINOIS,
MORGAN County, } ss.

The People of the State of Illinois to EARL HEMBROUGH, SHERIFF , GREETING:

You are hereby commanded forthwith to apprehend

JOHN DOE

who has been declared to be a feeble-minded person, and to deliver h. im to the superintendent of

Lincoln State School and Colony at Lincoln, Illinois, without unnecessary delay, and of this warrant

make due return to this office after its execution, with the receipt of the superintendent endorsed on the

back thereof.

WITNESS, my hand and the seal of the County Court of Morgan

County, Illinois, this 29th day of October, A. D. 1945

Geo F. Douglas
Clerk of the County Court.

The commitment order that sent John away

LINCOLN STATE SCHOOL AND COLONY
ADMISSION BLANK

19325
3-192.

Name John Doe No. 2 Date October 30, 1945
County Morgan Religion County or private
Correspondent Picked up in Jacksonville
Ill. deaf-mute. No information

Admission Readmission Return from parole
By whom Tom O'Connell Deputy Sheriff
Age Height Weight
Hair D. Brown Eyes D. Brown Complexion Dark (Negro)
Remarks No information
Deputy Sheriff states Good natured, good
worker if understands what is wanted
(Signed) Officer of the Day
Bertha B. Duff

The official form that admitted John into the Lincoln State
School and Colony, 30 October 1945

SUMMARY OF PSYCHOLOGICAL EXAMINATION

Case No. 19325

Name	Birth Date	Date
DOE, JOHN #2	unknown	11-17-45

Reactions During Examination   Initial:

Patient is somewhat undernourished Negro male about whom no information is available. He was picked up on the streets of Jacksonville and committed to this institution because he was a deaf mute and could not read or write. Because of these factors and because whereabouts of his family are not know, no information about him can be obtained. He cooperated well in the test situation and seemed to understand instructions fairly well. His behavior on the ward is not satisfactory. He is destructive and tries to remove screens from windows apparently in an attempt to escape. It is reported that he frequently engages in masturbatory activities.

Psychological Findings   His mental age on the Arthur Performance Test, 6-10, resulting in an IQ of 43. The chronological age of 16 was used since it appears that this patient is at least 16 years old although his age cannot be verified. With the exception of relatively good score on the Casuist

~~Stanford-Binet~~

C.A.	Arthur Performance 16
M.A.	6-10
I.Q.	43

Educational Ability   (SEE BACK)

Apparently illiterate.

Orientation

Undetermined.

Social Reactions

Cooperative, fairly pleasant.

Classification

Imbecile--upper division

Recommendation

Industrialization; general social group training.

Signed _R.D. Cutts_

Psychologist

General description of John and the results of his IQ test, which were given to him shortly after he was committed to the Lincoln State School

The Lincoln State School was virtually a self-contained town. It included its own power plant *(above)* for generating electricity. Courtesy Lincoln Developmental Center.

Dining hall at the Lincoln State School. Courtesy Lincoln Developmental Center.

The farm at the Lincoln State School, at nearly one thousand acres, was a major agricultural operation. Powered by the free labor provided by thousands of patients, the farm produced corn, oats, alfalfa, and clover. It also had a prize-winning dairy herd. Courtesy Lincoln Developmental Center.

The Lincoln State School cannery processed the crops harvested at the farm. Several thousand cans of food were produced each year. Courtesy Lincoln Developmental Center.

Aerial views of the Lincoln Developmental Center in the mid-1970s. The E-shaped buildings were the residences for the patients. Courtesy Lincoln Developmental Center.

John at a Springfield group home, ca. 1983. Courtesy
Mary Haas Doehring.

PEORIA ASSOCIATION FOR RETARDED CITIZENS

Personal Funds Management

As Legal guardian/responsible party of _John Boyd_ , I
hereby authroize _Barbara P. Smith_ _Tenter_ to manage a checking
(facility's name)

and/or savings account for my son/daughter.

I authorize the Administrator, or his/her designee, to withdraw if necessary,
the following routine amounts from _Saving & Checking_ account
without prior approval. I realize this will enable residents to be more independent
in community based outings and activities, as well as allow increased staff
time for programming. This agreement can be changed and/or updated at bi-annual
staffings. By allowing this choice of payment, I realize this will mean I will
not be notified of routine community outings and/or personal purchases that
I have already agreed to.

1. Cost of care
2. Cablevision (that has been previously agreed to)
3. Weekly allowances
4. Telephone expenses
5. Hygiene supplies (not to exceed $15.00 monthly)
   Medical supplies (not covered by Medicaid)

ITEM	MAXIMUM AMOUNT
Out House Activities	
Weekly Allowance	
ITEM	MAXIMUM AMOUNT
ITEM	MAXIMUM AMOUNT
ITEM	MAXIMUM AMOUNT
ITEM	MAXIMUM AMOUNT

Resident: _____ Date: _1-9-91_

Guardian: _____ Date: _____

Responsible Party: _____ Date: _____

Advocate: X _Harold H. Fowler_ Date: _1-9-91_

Facility Representative: _Shelby M. Wilson_ Date: _1-9-91_

Form No: _____

Date: _____

John's scrawling of his name after the word "Resident" on his personal
funds management form. Nursing home employees in Peoria interpreted
this as "Lewis."

UNKNOWN SINCE '45, JOHN DOE TAKES HIS SECRET TO THE GRAVE

Jacksonville, Ill., Dec. 4 (AP)

The mystery of John Doe No. 24 outlived him.

There were few clues when he was found wandering the streets of Jacksonville in 1945, a deaf, blind teen-ager. There were no answers when he died last week.

He was unable to speak, his relatives could not be found and he was put in an institution. He became John Doe No. 24 because he was the 24th unidentified man in the state's mental health system.

Officials believe he was 64 when he died of a stroke last Sunday at the Sharon Oaks nursing home in Peoria.

"It's just sad to think that you could disappear, and no one would miss you," said Glenn W. Miller, the nursing home administrator. "You wonder how often it happens."

The man's caretakers believe diabetes made him lose his sight, and records indicate he was severely retarded. But workers at the Smiley Living Center in Peoria, where he spent the last six years of his life, remember a proud man, more intelligent than standard tests showed.

They remembered the tantalizing hints to his identity—the way he would scrawl "Lewis" and his pantomimed, wild accounts of foot-stomping jazz bars and circus parades.

"It was so obvious from what he pantomimed that he had quite a life at one time," said Kim Cornwell, a caseworker. "Like a grandfather, he could probably tell funny stories. We just couldn't reach out enough to get them."

Straw Hat and Backpack

After he was found in Jacksonville, John Doe No. 24 spent 30 years at the Lincoln Developmental Center, a state home in Lincoln. He was then transferred several times before going to the Smiley home in 1987.

He had a straw hat he loved to wear, and he took a backpack with his collection of rings, glasses and silverware with him everywhere. At Christmas parties he danced to vibrations from the music.

Last Christmas the staff at Smiley bought gifts for residents who did not have relatives or other visitors. They bought him a harmonica.

In August he had surgery for colon cancer. When he came back from the hospital, he had trouble eating and was depressed. He was transferred to the nursing home in October.

At a brief graveside service last Wednesday in Jacksonville, a woman asked if anyone had any words to say. No one did.

Reprinted with Permission by Associated Press

Associated Press news story on John's death. The whereabouts of John's hat, harmonica, and other personal effects are unknown. By permission of the Associated Press.

John's grave in Peoria with the stone purchased by Mary Chapin Carpenter. The inscription is from her song, "John Doe No. 24." It reads, "life's a mystery, but so too is the human heart." Photo by Judy Lutz.

5 Learning How to Live: New York, 1981–1983

He was certainly a special person. People really loved him. They were drawn
to him for some reason. He had the smile. He put that grin on.
—Sue Ruzenski, Helen Keller Center

The Helen Keller Center

At an intake meeting held a couple of weeks before John arrived in New
York, the Helen Keller staff learned that John was fairly independent but
needed help on his communication skills and his ability to perform simple
tasks. In planning a program for John, staff members took into account
the fact that he had been institutionalized for thirty-five years and would
show some unacceptable behavior. Jealously guarding all of his possessions
may have been necessary in Lincoln, but if John were to assimilate into
the "outside world," he would need to be taught to relax.

When John and Willie had arrived at the Helen Keller Center, the staffers met with them to learn about John's personality and any other important facts about him that would help them communicate with him and
make him feel at ease. John, they were told, could bathe himself, but he
used soap instead of shampoo to wash his hair. That was something he
had learned in Lincoln, where shampoo was scarce. One of the first goals
set for John was to get him to use shampoo. In teaching him that, the Helen
Keller staff learned about John's ability to use his voice. He had command
of a range of sounds with which he could express his displeasure. They ranged
from a gruff "Hunhhh" and a scowl to a full-throated, angry bellow.

The Helen Keller Center consisted of two main buildings. The residence
hall contained small, dormitorylike rooms. John's room had two single beds
(he had no roommate), a closet, and a bathroom. His room was on the first
floor at the end of a hall, just next to the door leading outside. He had to

93

go out of his room and to the left to get anywhere but outside. There were bars along the walls, but John still preferred to "trail" his fingers along the wall to keep his bearings. On the floor just before each flight of steps was a rough pad. When the residents felt the pad with their feet, they knew they were arriving at stairs.

The other building, roughly a fifty-yard walk across the grounds, was where most of John's instruction would take place. It also contained a gymnasium, the secretarial pool, and the center's administrative offices.

As it was in Jacksonville, the center had mostly tile floors and block walls with stainless steel bars along them. The house rule was to always keep to the right when walking down the halls.

Peter Krienbihl was among the group that met John and Willie at La-Guardia. Peter was an aide on the 3:00 to 11:00 P.M. shift in the center's residence building. Peter noticed soon after John arrived that John clung to what he had learned in Jacksonville and resisted any new information that the Helen Keller staff tried to teach him. Peter believed that John's scope of knowledge, even his institutional behavior, was a source of pride to him. It wasn't as if John were purposely being difficult. This was the way he had learned to live. This is what he was comfortable with.

Joseph McNulty, residence director of Helen Keller when John arrived, didn't need to look in the files to see that John had been in an institution for a long time. McNulty saw the unmistakable signs that those years had left on John. There was John's tendency to hoard whatever he could find and claim as his own. John was also accustomed to taking whatever he wanted. Things just seemed to disappear whenever he was around. If he found something that interested him, he put it in his pocket.

Whenever John went outside, he felt around him until he found a coat. When he found one, he put it on. It didn't matter that it wasn't his coat. It was a coat. That's the way it had been done in Lincoln. He was the same way about shoes. If he found some that came close to fitting him, he wore them.

A week or two before John arrived, social worker Bob Ackerman talked with the staff who would be working with John. John's strengths and weaknesses were discussed at this "pre-intake meeting," as it was called at the center. Much of John's background information from Lincoln and Jacksonville that had been shipped to New York was disregarded by the Helen Keller staff. The "severe retardation" diagnosis that was a part of his makeup in Lincoln and Jacksonville was never taken seriously in New York.

It wasn't that the center's staff members thought the people who had cared for John before them didn't know what they were doing. But experience with people who came to them from institutions had taught them that records could be deceiving. The Helen Keller staff preferred to find out for itself how much a new client was capable of accomplishing.

He Is His Own Man

Sue Ruzenski was director of the Daily Living Skills Department at Helen Keller in 1983. The purpose of the department was to teach clients the fundamentals of living. The goal for John, which was decided upon before he even arrived in New York, was to prepare him for a life outside of an institution.

Daily Living Skills taught John how to care for himself, manage his personal things, enjoy his leisure time, and improve his dining skills and toileting. The staff was in John's room, teaching him how to groom himself as soon as he got out of bed at 7:15 A.M. John awoke at that time each day with the help of a James Remind-O-Timer by his bed. The device worked by vibrating the bed when the alarm went off. The alarm could be set by the blind by having them feel pegs that corresponded in location to the numbers on a clock face. At first, the clock was set for him, but John eventually learned to feel the pegs until he arrived at the time he wanted. Then he simply moved the peg in. Halfway in meant half past the hour. All the way meant on the hour. For some of the male residents, the quick vibration of the bed in the morning was sexually arousing and an opportune time for masturbation. John's sex drive, however, was virtually gone, probably a result of his diabetes medication or the years of psychotropic drugs. When his bed shook, he simply got up. At times, he needed extra prompting. When a staff member had to come in to shake him awake, John usually growled. But he got up.

As he went through his morning routine of washing, dressing, and brushing his teeth, a staffer was right next to him to teach him the hand-on-hand signs for those activities.

The Helen Keller staff taught all its residents that there was only one way to make a bed, and that was the way they were required to do it each time. It was the same with brushing their teeth. There was a right way and a wrong way to do that, too. For better or worse, the staff members believed that they knew what was the right way for their clients to live. (That somewhat arrogant approach would eventually give way to a more flexible attitude that respected the fact that clients had their own way of accomplishing things.)

Sue found out, as Peter had, that John already knew how to do some of the tasks he was supposed to learn in Daily Living Skills. He just didn't do them by the book. And he had trouble getting motivated. In the past, John had been able to get around certain tasks. In Lincoln, it was because the staff was hopelessly outnumbered by patients. In Jacksonville, he was allowed to sit and do nothing on his free time. But that all ended at Helen Keller. There would be no breaks for John in New York.

His room was laid out almost exactly opposite from the way his room in Jacksonville was designed. In his first weeks in New York, John kept running into the closet door when he was trying to find the bathroom. It took two months for him to figure out the new arrangement.

It was easier for him to learn the way to the cafeteria and to the other places where he would be spending his time. He could not travel across an open space, especially outside, without assistance. He relied so much on his sense of touch that he was lost without a wall nearby to use as a guide. He could cross an open room once he learned its layout.

John was assigned a locker in the training building. He stored his coat and his cane there. Mary Ransdell would have been surprised to see that, in New York, John readily accepted the cane. Helen Keller residents were not allowed to use their canes indoors, but John found it helpful to use one in getting from one building to the other.

When John was escorted to the training building each morning, the first thing he did was go to his locker. He knew the door of the locker room because it had the handle of a locker glued to it. The staff put a sandpaper-covered *J* on John's locker door and on the door of his dorm room so that he could easily identify them.

Work began again on teaching John to associate simple signs with an object. It started with food. Whenever John ate something, the staff gave him the sign for it.

The staff made up a menu for John. Every day, he drank coffee for breakfast, tea for lunch, and tea for dinner. He seemed to enjoy it and didn't complain.

About seven months after he arrived, John sat down for lunch. He felt for the tea bag that he knew would be in his cup. But, this day, instead of simply drinking his tea as usual, John did something different. He dropped his tea bag onto the table, pushed the cup away, shouted to get someone's attention, and approximated the sign for coffee.

Sister Bernadette Wynne, a staff member of Helen Keller, said it was the first sign, other than "bathroom," that the staff had seen John use without prompting. Someone rushed his tea cup away and came back with a cup of coffee. John felt the cup and fished around in it with his spoon. He found no tea bag. He raised the cup and smelled it. Once he was convinced it was coffee, he drank it happily.

John soon realized that if he learned the sign for something to eat, he could get it. Now, no matter what meal the staff gave him, he wanted something else. More language was spilling out of him than the Helen Keller staff knew he had.

Sometimes, it seemed as if the plane ride to New York had given John amnesia. Mary Ransdell had taught John the sign for "coffee" years ago in Jacksonville. He knew how to ask for coffee when he was there, but at the Helen Keller Center he had to be taught the sign again. Perhaps it was because New York was a new place. John had learned in his first week in Lincoln, nearly forty years before coming to New York, that the communication signs he had known previously were useless. Every new place had new signs for him to learn.

Until he came to know and, what is more important, trust the staff at Helen Keller, John would not use his signs there. After the experience in the dining room, the staff knew that there was a load of ability locked up inside John that he wasn't ready to share. When he began to feel comfortable, it connected somewhere in his brain that if he did start to use his signs, the staff would understand what he was trying to say. In the other places he had been, only a few people would understand his signs. He could be signing "coffee" all day, and they wouldn't understand it. Now that the staff members at Helen Keller knew how much John liked coffee, they taught him to make it himself.

When John was walking with Peter one day, John casually blew his nose into his hand. Peter made a mental note: "We need to teach John to use a handkerchief." John could learn in a short time how to use those things, like a handkerchief, that made sense to him. It also helped if someone he liked, such as Peter, was the one to teach him.

John didn't warm up to the staff in his first few months at Helen Keller. He did not understand why he was in a new place with new people. He may have thought being sent to this new place was some kind of punishment. While he was in the process of deciding whether he liked the staff members or whether any of them could be trusted, he decided to keep to himself.

John had apparently decided long before coming to the Helen Keller Center that he did not need to use American Sign Language. Even though he had the mental capacity to understand it, he preferred his own method of communication. He knew he could express himself without using the "official" signs. There were a few things for which he might use a sign. But it usually upset him when the Helen Keller staff insisted that he use the proper signs.

John had also developed a wide range of sounds that he used to express himself. Like a baby that can't talk, he had his happy sounds, angry sounds, frustrated sounds, and even teasing sounds. He was getting better at communicating, but he was not a good signer. But between his vocalizations, his facial expressions, and his body language, the staff knew exactly what he was trying to say.

Each morning after he was dressed, John was led down the hall from his room to the cafeteria for breakfast. Now that he knew how to order whatever he wanted for a meal, and no one was going to steal his food, he found eating to be a pleasant experience. Since he was happy to go to the cafeteria, he was eager to learn how to get there. After breakfast, however, he wasn't as cooperative. He was to return to his room and get his coat before walking across the grounds to the training building. But John could not understand why he had to go back to his room, get a coat, go back down the hall again and out the door. He would rather take the first coat he found, put it on, and go. There was a fight over the coat every day. The staff came to expect it.

John received $347.51 a month in Supplemental Security Income from Social Security. He also received Medicaid checks from the state of New York. Out of that money, he paid $180.00 a week to the Helen Keller Center in room, board, and tuition. He had enough left over to put some in an account kept for him by the staff.

Residents were also given a weekly allowance. They could use their money to buy whatever they wanted on weekly shopping trips. John was encouraged to spend his money on toiletries, but he resisted. He didn't want to spend any money.

Money, he knew, was valuable. It could bring him pleasure in the form of cigarettes or peanuts, two of his favorite treats. But he only liked coins. Mary Ransdell's lessons in Jacksonville had started with coins and only later progressed to paper money. The money he earned in Jacksonville was usually in nickels, dimes, and quarters. As a result, John was most familiar with the value of coins.

He wadded his coins into the handkerchiefs Peter brought him. Then he stuffed the coin-filled handkerchiefs into his pants pockets. It was a familiar sight to see John walking the halls at Helen Keller with his pants down around his hips—weighed down by as many pennies, nickels, dimes, and quarters as he could stuff into his pockets. The staff, concerned that his pants would just fall down someday, finally gave him a coin box and encouraged him to keep his money in it.

At night, he was allowed to lock his coin box into a night stand by his bed. It sounded like a good idea but quickly became a major project. Being blind, John couldn't figure out how the key had to go into the lock. It was frustrating for him and the staff. When he eventually conquered the riddle of key and lock, he was methodical about his coin box. Every night, John took out the money he had crammed into his pockets, opened the box, put the coins in, and locked it up. In the morning, he took it all out again and put it back into his pockets.

John discovered that some of the residents at the center did not lock the doors to their rooms. John learned to "trail" down the wall of the residence area until he came to a doorway. Then he tested the doors of the rooms. If they weren't locked, he turned his head from left to right, as if he were looking around. He swept his arm in an arc behind him to make sure there was no one near. If he felt no one, he went into the room and felt around for items he wanted. Of course, there was usually someone watching him. When he or she came in and tapped him on the shoulder, he either smiled as if to say, "OK, you caught me," or he growled angrily. It depended on his mood.

He picked up anything that was left lying around the Helen Keller Center. The staff had seen that behavior before in people who came from institutions. Those clients were used to having things they left lying around disappear, so they became hoarders. John always carried his treasures in his pockets. He was afraid that if he left anything alone, it wouldn't be there when he got back. Ironically, John was the one from whom the others had to protect their possessions.

Tools

Six people crowded into a corner of the small training kitchen at Helen Keller. Some were blind; some were therapists helping them to learn their way around the kitchen. They could barely move without running into each other.

John was wearing his usual "uniform" of jeans, a sport shirt, and a sweat suit jacket. The handkerchiefs stuffed with coins protruded from his pockets. He walked slowly, with a stiff gait that looked like something from the movie *Night of the Living Dead*. It was time to teach John how to set a table for a meal.

Teaching John anything involved having him do the same tasks over and over. The staff was fighting to break through thirty-six years of institutional habits. For all but a few of those years, John's education and growth as a person were ignored. Teaching him now was that much more difficult. It was repetitive, frustrating, intense, and time-consuming work.

In the training kitchen, John felt gingerly for a cupboard door down at knee level. He bent, then bent lower, always searching with his fingers for the door handle. Sue Ruzenski was beside him, watching his progress. Ruzenski finally took his hand and guided it to the cupboard handle. John opened it and took out four plastic placemats. Sue signed in John's hand that he was to take the mats to the kitchen table. She held his left arm as he made his way across the room. He strayed off course on his way to the table, so she put his hand against the corner of the wall until he got his bearings. Then he moved forward again. He found the table first with his thigh and then with his hands.

John put the four placemats haphazardly on the table. Sue, by putting John's hand from the mat to the edge of the table, showed him that he was to put them flush with the edge. John felt for the edge, then lined the mats with it neatly. He put one upside down. Sue put his hand on the mat and showed him that there was a smooth side and a rough side. The smooth side went up. He corrected his mistake.

There was a tray with cups already on the table. Sue put John's hand on it, then moved his hand to the center of the table, back to the cups, then back to the center. She was letting him know that he must put the cups in the middle of the table. He understood what she wanted and accomplished it immediately. Sue then led him back to the cupboards.

Now he was told to get some bowls. He took them from another cupboard, then put them on a tray. Once that was done, he leaned against a wall as if he were done for the day. Sue made him understand otherwise. She signed "fork" in his hand. John had difficulty getting the utensils out of their drawer but eventually collected enough for four place settings. He identified each utensil by running his finger along the handle to the tines or knife edge or spoon bowl. He put the silverware on a tray with some orange, green, and brown bowls.

The training kitchen was so crowded and cramped that the blind clients were frequently bumping into each other. As John turned with his tray full of bowls and silverware, he ran into a woman. Nothing spilled to the floor, but he stood statue-still until the path was cleared. Sue guided him back to the table. He put the tray down and, either thinking he was done or tired of this exercise, turned to leave. Sue stopped him. She signed "napkin." He felt along the table until he found a napkin holder, then pulled two napkins out. He noticed that he had one too many and stuffed the extra one back in the holder. He put the napkin on the placemat in front of him, then leaned back again, hoping to be done. Sue got him started on the task again. She would not allow him to slide.

This time, John put the napkin in the center of the mat. She showed him his mistake and directed his hand to the edge of the mat, then back to the napkin, then back to the edge. He understood and moved the napkin to its proper place. He took two more napkins and walked to the other side of the table. He laid them on the placemats and waited for more instructions from Sue.

She guided him back around the table to the tray with silverware. He located on it a knife, fork, and spoon but didn't seem to know what to do with them. He stood holding them and doing nothing. Sue stepped up to him and moved his hand to the placemat. On the first placemat, John put the knife and spoon on the right, the fork on the left. He took three more utensils and moved to the next place at the table. But someone was sitting there. He was confused. It was the same blind woman whom he bumped into with his tray. She felt John standing next to her and touched his arm. Sue, hovering very near John, was quickly there and directed John to put the silverware on the placemat.

Back at the tray for another place setting, John picked up two spoons by mistake. Sue showed him what he had done, and he put down the spoon and picked up a fork. He walked to the other side of the table, put the knife on the left and the fork and spoon on the right. Again, Sue showed him his mistake, and he corrected it.

At the last place setting, John got it right the first time. He started to put the knife on the left but caught himself and put the fork there. But his lesson in table setting was still not over.

He was guided back to his tray for some bowls. He felt them with his hands but didn't do anything with them. Sue placed his hand back on the bowls. He picked one up and held it out to her. She led his hand to a placemat. John set the bowl on top of the knife and spoon. Sue directed him to move it to the center of the mat. John placed the next three bowls perfectly. At last, he was finished.

The process of setting four places at the table took about half an hour. It wasn't as if he had never done it before. By the time he left Jacksonville, Mary Ransdell had already taught him to set the table. But the lesson seemed lost in the transition so must be learned again. John would do it all again tomorrow.

After observing John for about a year, and having varying success in overcoming his institutional behavior, the question became whether the staff members should force John to do things "the right way" or let him do things the way he had learned to do them. They decided they would allow John to use the rough skills he had when he arrived and concentrated, instead, on teaching him new ones.

If one used the 1929 birth year the authorities gave him in 1945, John was fifty-two when he arrived at the Helen Keller Center. The staff was learning that it was a losing battle to attempt to "unteach" him what he had learned.

The goal set for John, even before he arrived at the center, was to ensure that he never had to spend another day in an institution. Staff members were determined to teach him enough that he could get by in a group home.

John had a tendency to be lazy. He needed to be prodded by the staffers to stay awake or to work at the skills they were trying to teach him. If left alone, he was content to sit by himself and do nothing but smoke and eat peanuts.

Now the staffers woke him at 7:00 A.M. and had him working right away. They brought him to the training building for a full day of classes and then had him work some more when he returned to the residence building. John was jolted by all of the attention and demands on him, demands he could not get out of. He was often reluctant and expressed it by growling or complaining or being stubbornly resistant to what the staff wanted him to do. But, despite his reluctance, he was constantly learning something new.

He soon learned how to do his laundry. That came relatively easy. It began with teaching John that when he took his clothes off at the end of the day, they went in a certain place. When the staff decided it was time for him to wash them, he carried the basket of clothes to the laundry room. There, an aide used hand-over-hand signs to tell him to put the clothes in the washing machine and put in the soap. Someone put John's hand on the control dials. Each dial had raised knobs to indicate time.

Most of the residents wanted to learn to use the washing machines, not so much because they were fastidious about clean clothes, but because they loved to feel the machine vibrate. When the washer or dryer was going, many residents would put their faces and hands on it to feel it shake.

The staff used a system of safety pins to help residents differentiate between "colors" and "whites" in their laundry. John, however, would feel the safety pin and, instead of knowing it was something colored, remove the pin because he didn't think it should be there.

John didn't readily embrace the notion of doing laundry, but he realized that he had to do it. He used to go to bed with his clothes on. Peter or another staff member would see him sleeping in his clothes and wake him up and sign, "No, that's wrong," into his hand. They made him get out of bed, put on pajamas, and put his dirty clothes into the laundry basket. As the days passed, John's dirty clothes basket became fuller and his closet became emptier. His solution was to take his dirty clothes out of the basket and wear them again. But the staff stopped him from doing that. Then, when all of his underwear were dirty, he tried putting on his jeans with no underwear. He wasn't allowed to do that, either.

Eventually, the system started to make sense to John. He apparently reached a point when he said to himself, "OK, they're making me do this. I don't have a choice. I'm not allowed to wear these dirty clothes. They must be laundered. And not only are they making me do this, but I know how to do it myself. So I might as well do it." As he learned to do more things, he became less of a high-maintenance client who needed assistance with everything.

He also began to understand that if he went along with what the staff members wanted, he could ask them for something, like coffee, and receive it. To John, a cup of coffee and a cigarette was like a relaxing walk in the park would be to a tired office worker. But, unlike the walk in the park, the experience of smoking a cigarette is something a blind, deaf person can enjoy as much as a sighted person. It is a sensual experience, not a visual or auditory one. The smell of it, the feel of the smoke being drawn into the lungs and back out—all of it is a sensory feast.

Eating a peanut provided the same tactile enjoyment. John could crack the shell himself and eat a peanut with no assistance. Nobody had to cook it for him. Even with a cigarette, John needed someone to light it for him. Eating a peanut was one of the few things he could do entirely by himself.

At the time John was at the center, smoking was allowed in the TV lounge. John still preferred to sit apart from the others. He had gained weight since coming to New York, so he usually unbuttoned his jeans after he sat down. When he smelled the smoke from a nearby cigarette, he would hold up two fingers and grunt, indicating that he would like a smoke, too. Very early in the evening, sometimes as early as 5:30 or 6:00, he rose from his chair, walked to his room, and went to bed.

The Third Farewell

On Friday mornings, a large group from the center ate breakfast at a deli and then went shopping. John sometimes went with them. When John had finished eating, he would stand and make sounds and gestures, indicating that he wanted a cigarette.

The group shopped at a McCrory's, a small discount store on Long Island. The only reason John consented to go, the staff believed, was because he knew he could buy cigarettes and peanuts at McCrory's. On trips to the store, John carried the Helen Keller Center version of a shopping list—a tote bag full of trash—with him. When John was out of cigarettes, a staff member would throw the empty pack into the bag. When he ran out of toothpaste, the empty tube was put into the bag. By the time John went to the store, the bag was full of empty cartons, tubes, and packages. While John was in the store, he had only to open his tote bag and feel the items inside to know what he needed to buy. He insisted on getting cigarettes and peanuts first.

Whenever he felt an empty toothpaste tube or shampoo bottle in his bag, John became angry. He didn't want to spend his money on those things. He had always received them for free until he came to this new place. Why, he wondered, didn't they get them for him? Why should he have to spend his money, his most precious possession, on something he considered virtually unnecessary? The staff resorted to throwing those two items into John's shopping cart without his knowledge. But at the store checkout, he was the one who took the items out of his cart and put them on the checkout line conveyor belt. When he realized the toothpaste and shampoo were in his cart anyway, he complained loudly about being charged for those things. It was embarrassing to have John standing at the checkout, bellowing and shouting in anger. Eventually, the staff snuck either the toothpaste or the shampoo into the cart but gave up on trying to do both. The center staff eventually resorted to rewarding John with peanuts, sourballs, cigarettes, or raisins if he would spend his money on shampoo and toothpaste.

Some of the deaf-blind residents at the center were extremely defensive. The slightest touch or bump could provoke them into violence. When John was in certain moods, he could express his anger physically. But that was not his usual method. Once he got to know the people who were working with him, he was relatively easy to handle. He could even charm the staff when he was having a good day. Considering his background, the center's employees expected him to be morose and sullen. But his pride wouldn't let that happen.

He had a sense of humor, but he wouldn't show it to just anyone. John was able to identify the people with whom he would simply be cooperative and those to whom he would give a little more of himself—sometimes he gave them a little too much. Sue Ruzenski noticed that John sometimes stood inappropriately close to the female residents and staff and even touched them or ran his hands over their bodies. And then he'd laugh. It was obvious that he knew what he was doing. It would only happen once in a while, when John was in a certain mood.

On the next day, he could be cold and hard to reach again. On those days, he wouldn't want to be bothered by anybody—men or women—whether he knew them or not.

By late 1982, the Helen Keller staff determined that John had reached the goal that had been set for him. It was determined that he could be discharged from the institution and function in a supervised group home. After nearly forty years of being in the care of trained (and untrained) psychologists, therapists, teachers, and doctors, he was ready to enter mainstream society. He was ready to leave. But where would he go and to what?

John was still officially a ward of the state of Illinois. He was only discharged from the Jacksonville Developmental Center so that he could go to New York. They always assumed he would come back to Illinois when his time was up. Now that it was time, the Illinois Department of Mental Health searched hard for an appropriate group home for John. It contacted Springfield Aid to Retarded Citizens, which was just beginning to use the group home concept. That organization had trained married couples who would act as supervisors to three or four, sometimes more, mentally disabled people who lived with them. They said they would find a place for John.

John had arrived in New York with relatively few independent skills. But through adding new skills to what John already knew, they had brought him as close as he would ever be to a man who could live his life without help.

In his two years at the center, he had been taught to fold his clothes and put them in the proper drawers; collect the material for dusting furniture and complete the job; plug in and use a vacuum cleaner; shine his shoes; file his nails; use a clothes washer and dryer; and prepare a breakfast of orange juice, coffee, and toast. He had even learned to spend money.

Over the previous two years, John had made his adjustment to Helen Keller. Now he would have to leave. He would begin the transition process once again. It frustrated the staffers to put John in that position again, but doing so was what they'd been working toward.

The center's residents reacted to being put into new and unfamiliar situations in different ways. The Helen Keller staff had seen biting, kicking, and other forms of assaultive behavior. But even the most violent had eventually found someone on the staff with whom they could bond. And, like John, they were "rewarded" for their cooperation by being sent away. One of the staff's goals was to get clients to a point at which their language and understanding were good enough that by the time they left, they realized why they were going. That reduced the frustration level somewhat. But "goodbye day" was still hard on the clients, as well as on the staff who had not only come to know them but had seen them make great strides in their abilities.

It was a memorable day when John left. After two years, a longer-than-normal stay at Helen Keller, he had become a fixture. He had shown staff members that he could connect with the people he'd met there. In his way, he felt close to them, as close as he would let himself get. They worried now about how John would handle going back to Illinois. But they knew that by this time in his life—he was probably in his fifties—John had seen so many people come and go that he probably wouldn't be as sad as they were when he left.

The staff members wondered whether there was more they could do with John. They believed they had only been able to bring out a little of John's ability, and he could have been capable of doing more if they had spent more time with him. But his time was up. He needed to go on to the next step.

They threw a party for John when he left on 11 July 1983. Some of the staff regarded him as one of the most memorable people who had attended the center.

Most clients of the Helen Keller Center were accompanied by a staff member when they left. The staffer helped the client's family and the client adjust to the transition period. In John's case, it was decided that Peter Krienbihl would go back to Illinois with him. Peter's job was to help the managers of John's group home understand how to communicate with John, tell them of his habits and personality, and make sure that John was going into a situation that was good for him.

It took some persuasion before John would take all of his "treasure" out of his room. He wanted it to stay right where he'd hidden it. But the staff knew he would want it back in Springfield, so John finally jammed everything that wouldn't fit into his cash box into his pockets. What he couldn't fit into his pants, he put into his coat pockets.

Peter was walking through the metal detector at the airport when he suddenly realized that John, who was right behind him, was going to make the metal detector go crazy. It went off right on cue, as John walked through. He, of course, heard nothing and just kept walking. He was surprised and greatly annoyed when airport security personnel stopped him. When they tried to check his pockets, he was furious, and he resisted.

Peter explained the situation to the security officers. He told them that John would never let them examine his pockets. They would, he said, just have to trust him. The airport security force wouldn't go quite that far, but they were willing to compromise by feeling the outside of John's pockets. John was unhappy with that but had no choice. He moaned, and he groaned, but he did not, as Peter feared he would, take a swing at anyone.

John and Peter were running late by the time they reached their gate. They were taking a smaller jet back to Illinois. This was the first time Peter had ever flown in an airplane. He was convinced that he was the more nervous of the two.

The flight from New York to St. Louis was uneventful. But when John and Peter arrived at Lambert Field, they transferred to an even smaller plane, a commuter flight to Champaign. Seeing the size of the plane, jokingly referred to by some passengers as "the tube of death," was not easy on Peter's pulse or blood pressure. The commuter plane, however, arrived safely in Champaign.

Being in the middle of corn country was another shock to Peter, a New Yorker to his bones. He was in awe of the space and its flatness. He didn't have much time to look around before the plane was taxiing down the runway again. He grabbed the armrest of his seat and hoped for the best. As the plane left the ground, he glanced at John to see how he was coping with the flight. He found that John was rather enjoying himself, sitting in his seat just as cool as if he were the pilot.

6 Independence: Springfield, 1983–1987

John was capable of a lot more than anyone ever gave him credit for. He had a lot inside of him for caring for people, a lot.
—Mary Haas Doehring, John's group home manager, Springfield

Another Mary

Mary Haas and her husband, Ken, ran the first Community Residential Alternative home established in Springfield by the city's Aid to Retarded Citizens (ARC). Their group home was on South College, a residential area in the south central part of Springfield. It was a small home in which ARC clients could live as an alternative to being institutionalized. When John arrived, the Haases had two ARC clients, Mike and Bill, already living with them.

When the Haases' group home was described to the Jacksonville Developmental Center's staff members, they were enthusiastic. They relayed the news to the Helen Keller Center, whose staff was equally excited. After fifty-two years of being in one facility or another, John was being released into as close to a private setting as he could get.

However, nobody was sure that the Haases would also think having a blind, deaf, and mute man come to live with them would be a good idea. John's multiple handicaps meant that those who took responsibility for him were letting themselves in for a lot of work. That being the case, Ken and Mary Haas were given a choice whether they wanted to take John in. Mike and Bill, their other two boarders, had simply been assigned to them. Mike and Bill were much younger than John and didn't have the multiple handicaps that John did.

In meetings at the Springfield ARC office, doctors and social workers didn't sugarcoat the situation for the Haases. John, they were told, was deaf, blind, diabetic, sometimes physically aggressive, couldn't speak, could barely communicate, could only perform a few household tasks for himself, and had severe arthritis. He knew sixty signs by the time he left Helen Keller but used about forty of them regularly. He also, the Haases were told, had substantial negative behavior that was so ingrained in him from his years in institutions that he would never lose it. Given all of that, the Haases were asked if they were still interested.

Ken and Mary knew that accepting John into their home would be risky. They were concerned that adding him to the group might upset the relationship they had built between themselves and Mike and Bill. But they also knew that if they didn't take John, he would probably have to go back to the developmental center in Jacksonville. The Haases saw John's records from New York and knew how far he had progressed in the last two years. They decided that John had come too far to go back to living in the state's mental health system. They could not deny him his only chance at a life outside the state's care. They told Springfield ARC officials that they would take him.

The Haases had already received training in the care of the disabled before they were allowed to take ARC clients into their home. Now that John was coming, they received more training, this time in hand-on-hand signing and other essentials they would need to know in order to take care of a person who was deaf and blind. At a local hospital, they met with dietitians who explained the requirements of John's diabetic diet. Nurses taught the Haases how to give John his daily insulin injections.

In going over John's records, the ARC staff found the name "John Doe Boyd" that Jacksonville's John Goebel had made up for him in order to get John a Social Security card. The ARC administrators decided that referring to John as either "John Doe Boyd" or just "John Boyd" would be more humane than calling him "John Doe." The Haases agreed.

When John's plane arrived at Capital Airport in Springfield, Mary and Ken were there to meet him. Peter Krienbihl led John off the plane and down the steps to the runway. That is where Mary and John were introduced.

"He will need a way to identify you," Peter told Mary, "some special way so that he knows it's you. Do you mind if he touches your face?"

Mary said she didn't mind. John touched her, gently moving his hands over her face to familiarize himself with it. He examined each line, fold, and bump of her face as if he were reading a book about her. As was his habit, he lingered at her earlobes. As he was concentrating on her, Mary was looking into his face and reading him as well.

"This man is very intelligent," she said to herself. "From what I've read about him, he's supposed to be severely retarded. I've only seen him for a few minutes, but I get the feeling he's not retarded at all."

When John had found whatever it was about Mary's face that would always identify her to him, he nodded at her and gave her a warm smile. "This," she thought, "is a man who just never had a chance."

When the Haases, John, and Peter arrived at the house on South College, John walked around inside, feeling everything as carefully as if he were going to buy it. Mary took him upstairs, where he would have his own bedroom and his own bathroom. The first things John searched for were the bed and the dresser. When he found the dresser, he opened a drawer and motioned for Peter. He wanted his cash box. Peter got it for him, and John put it in the drawer. Later, he hid the box's keys under his pillow.

Peter, as he looked around the home, was skeptical about how well John would adjust to it. Peter was acting like a father who had just brought his son to college and was appraising his dorm room. Peter cared about John, as did his fellow staff members at Helen Keller. They wanted Peter to make sure that John was going into a good situation. Peter wasn't so sure.

"This house is sort of like a land mine for him," Peter thought. "They have a lot of nice things hanging on the walls. This isn't 'proofed' for somebody who's blind. He's going to be bumping into things."

Peter noticed that John would have to negotiate steps to get to his room. He was sure John would have trouble doing that because of his arthritic condition. Inside John's bathroom, there were three more steps that led from the sink to the toilet.

Peter noticed immediately that Mike and Bill, the other two clients at the group home, were more lively than John preferred. "John's not going to like that," Peter thought. He wondered whether Mike or Bill would take advantage of John. That, in addition to his worries about the steps and John's unfamiliarity with the house's layout, made Peter skeptical that John could make a go of it in his new home.

The next day, it seemed that Peter's fears were going to be confirmed. As he and Ken and Mary were sitting downstairs, they heard shouting coming from John's room. Running up the stairs, they found John in a confused state, standing in a corner. Mary touched his shoulder, and he signed, "Where am I?"

He lost his bearings in the house numerous times those first few days. Whenever he did, he would shout for help, rather loudly, until someone found him. Then, on about his fourth day, John stayed in the house all day without getting lost.

When Mary had unpacked John's clothes, she noticed that his shirts were wrinkled. She washed them, then brought out her iron and some starch and made them crisp. When John put on his first freshly laundered shirt, he smiled broadly. From that day on, for as long as he was with the Haases, John would not wear a shirt unless it had been starched and ironed.

Mary had purchased a book on American Sign Language but soon found that it was useless. Instead, John began to teach Ken and Mary his own way of communicating. Most of the time, when John wanted to tell them something, his gestures were simple enough that they could understand them.

Within a week after arriving from New York, Peter returned to the Helen Keller Center. John, much to Peter's surprise, was adjusting well to the group home. John hadn't gotten lost inside the house in several days. The Haases were good to John, and it seemed that he liked them and would eventually learn to trust them. It was time for Peter to go.

On the day he left, Peter brought his suitcase downstairs to where John was sitting and stood before him. Peter, Ken, and Mary were worried about how John would react to Peter's departure. Peter was John's last link to New York and the people he trusted most at that time in his life. With Peter gone, John would be adrift again in a new world, without the comfort of anyone familiar to him.

"John," Peter signed to him, "I am leaving." He took John's hand and let him touch his suitcase so that he would understand what was happening.

John's reaction was to point to himself with a questioning look on his face. It was as if he were saying, "Me too?"

"No," Peter told him. "You stay here."

John wrinkled his brow and stood still, thinking about what was happening. After a few moments, he simply hugged Peter, turned on his heel, and went up to his room. Peter was just another one gone from his life. There had been many before him.

"I guess that's it," Mary said, and Peter headed for the door.

Telling Tales

It happened for the first time at an evening meal about four months after John arrived in Springfield. John said, "Aaaah, aaaaah," and made motions with his hands to get everyone's attention. He began to act out a story.

Ken and Mary were able to decipher some of it from the gestures and movements John made. It looked as if he were at a party. He imitated laughter and shook hands with imaginary people. And then he made some odd gestures that, nonetheless, Ken and Mary believed they understood. They looked at each other and laughed.

"Was that what I think it was?" Mary asked Ken.

"I think so," Ken said. "Wasn't he tapping a keg of beer?"

"That's sure what it looked like. I don't know what else it could have been. Where do you suppose he learned to do that?"

The Haases talked about John's storytelling episode for several days afterward. They wondered if they could have been wrong about the keg of beer. Was there anything else, they wondered, that involved similar motions? But John's pantomime was too good. The Haases kept returning to their original idea that he had been tapping a keg. He had pantomimed shoving the tap into the keg, pulling on the handle to draw the beer, and putting a glass under the spigot. When he acted out the same story again, the Haases wondered whether his parents may have owned a tavern when he was a child.

After he finished the story, Mary signed into his hand, "Where? When?" John made a motion with his arm indicating only that it happened "long ago."

John "told" other stories. He pretended to be in church with his hands folded in prayer. Another story was about fishing, and another was about going to a circus. For the lions and tigers in the circus story, John pantomimed roaring. He made an elephant's trunk and large ears appear by using his hands and arms. To portray a clown, he made the shape of a ball at his nose. For the ringmaster, John was a man with a top hat.

When Mary asked John how he learned about clowns, John again signed, "Long ago." Whenever the Haases asked John when a story had taken place or how he knew any of this, the answer was always the same: "Long ago."

The Haases tried to get John to tell stories of his life in Lincoln or Jacksonville. He never did. But he did give them something they thought was a clue to his past. They noticed that if someone put a piece of paper in front of John and a pen in his hand, he would make marks or try to write something. Occasionally, he wrote something on the paper that Ken and Mary said looked like the name "Tom."

"Do you think that's him?" Mary asked, "or is it someone from Lincoln, Jacksonville, or Helen Keller?"

Despite repeated questions, the Haases were never able to get the answers they wanted from John about his past. Either he had forgotten, or he didn't want to think about it anymore.

Mary and John arrived at a beauty shop in Springfield. Before they went in, Mary explained to John that he was about to get his hair cut. She lifted some of his hair and pretended to cut it. John nodded that he understood.

They went inside the shop, and John found a chair. Mary brought the hair stylist to John, and they shook hands. Mary wasn't sure how John was going to react to a haircut. She didn't get the chance to find out. Before the stylist even touched John's hair, he got up and walked away. Coaxing him into sitting down again was impossible.

"I'm sorry," an embarrassed Mary told the stylist. "Maybe he doesn't like your perfume or something."

Mary reported the problem to ARC. "What should I do?" she asked. "The man has to have his hair cut."

She was told to cut it herself. Mary already cut the hair of the other two clients living in the house. So she put John into a chair and explained to him that she was going to cut his hair—but just this one time. After this one time, she said, he would go to a barber or stylist. John sat perfectly still throughout his haircut. From then on, Mary was his barber.

Mary and John became friends. Since Mary's husband worked during the day, she was around John the most. That being the case, she came to understand his unorthodox ways of communicating. And she, like others before her, saw intelligence and dignity in John. She knew some small details of his life before coming to the group home—enough to know that it had been a hard life. And that, to her, was part of his appeal. He had been given great burdens to carry, and she thought he carried them gracefully.

Mary took John's hand in hers to tell him something. "John," Mary told him, "work. We go to work." John had been enrolled at the Bowden Adult Center, an educational program for ARC clients. The goal was to teach John to do simple manual labor. Sometimes the labor involved cutting and pasting. Other times, like at the old workshop in Jacksonville, John would perform basic assembly projects, such as screwing a bolt into a nut.

For the first couple of weeks John attended Bowden, Mary drove him there each day. She stayed with him all day for the first two days so that he would have a familiar person with him. Whenever John was put into a new situation, the first thing he wanted was to find one person he could trust. As long as that person assured him that the situation he was going into was safe, he would be cooperative. Mary was now that person for John. But after two days, she reduced her time with him to half a day.

Bill and Mike, the other two residents of the group home, had also befriended John. John especially liked and trusted Mike. Mike took the bus each morning to Bowden. Mary decided that it was time that John, too, rode the bus. She started the transition by walking with John and Mike to the bus stop. Soon, John allowed Mike to guide him to the bus without Mary. Each morning, John took Mike's arm as they left the house. Mike took great care to see that John got on and off the bus safely. When they arrived at the center, Mike walked John to the door to make sure John was all right. In the afternoon, Mike was on the bus when it arrived at Bowden. Mike always got off and helped John get on for the ride home.

For Mike, John represented some responsibility that he handled well. For John, Mike provided the security that he needed.

There was only one other blind student at the center. The staff had never worked with a deaf-blind-mute person. Fortunately, Ken Haas taught at Bowden and was able to teach the staff how to communicate with John.

One day in early May, John came home from the Bowden Center carrying something in his hand. With Mike guiding him, John proudly walked up to Mary and held out his hand. Mary took the card that was in it and looked at it. John had pasted together a Happy Mother's Day card and grinned as he gave it to Mary.

That's the Waltz: The Fourth Farewell

The radio was on—loud. The radio had large speakers that sent out waves of vibrations. John seemed to like it when it was played loud.

Mike and Bill were dancing wildly to the music. Then Ken and Mary joined them. The four of them were bouncing and jumping to the music, while John stood and swayed. Mary approached John, grabbed his arms, and tried to get him to dance. She kept dancing wildly and pulling on John to try to get him going.

"Nananananana," John said. Instead, he grabbed Mary's arms firmly and stopped her. That took her by surprise. Before she could do anything, John took her right arm and put it on his shoulder. He took her left hand in his right hand and raised his arm to shoulder level. His left arm went around her waist, and he began to dance with her. Mary stared at him in amazement as she let him lead her across the floor.

John and Mary danced together many times after that. John, Mary discovered, was a pretty good dancer. She just wasn't sure what dance he was doing. The next time Mary's mother, Pat, came to visit, Mary showed her the footwork John had done while they danced.

"What is that?" Mary asked her mother.

"Oh," Pat replied, "that's the waltz."

For the first four or five months he was with the Haases, John shouted angrily whenever he couldn't find something or was lost or when he was simply in a bad mood and didn't want to be bothered with anything. He eventually stopped shouting when he was upset, but he always got his message across. Perhaps he had decided he no longer needed to shout because he thought he had the Haases trained to understand his ways and his needs.

John became so comfortable with Mary that he even ventured a joke or two. While sitting in the waiting room at an ophthalmologist's office, John nudged Mary and motioned that he wanted a book that he had felt on a nearby table. Mary was surprised at the request but gave John the book because she was curious about what he was going to do with it.

John opened the book and sat as if he were reading it. Every few moments, he turned a page. Then he nudged Mary, motioned to the book, and laughed out loud.

The doctor's examination of John's eyes revealed a pressure buildup from the glaucoma. He was scheduled for laser surgery at Memorial Medical Center in Springfield. The doctor looked at John's records to get a history of his glaucoma. The records, still relying on the 1929 date the Jacksonville police had originally guessed for his year of birth, made John about fifty-five years old. But the doctor told Mary that, judging from his examination of John's eyes, he thought John might be as much as ten years older than that.

When John and Mary arrived at the hospital for the surgery, the nurses weren't sure how to handle John. Mary showed them how to approach him and told them to tap him gently on the shoulder and then lead him by the arm wherever they wanted him to go.

Mary arranged for a friend to stay with John at the hospital when Mary couldn't be there. One morning at 5:00 A.M., Mary's telephone rang. Her friend who was staying with John was calling.

"I've got an emergency at home, and I have to leave right away," she told Mary. "Can you come?"

"OK," Mary said. "I'm on my way."

When Mary arrived at Memorial, she went directly to John's room. But he wasn't there. She went to the nurses' station and asked about him. "He should be in his room," she was told. Mary and the nurses launched a frantic search for John in the hospital rooms and halls. They couldn't find him.

Mary returned to John's room and looked in his closet to see if his clothes were still there. They were. On a hunch, she opened the closet door of the other patient sharing the room. There, she found John sitting on the floor. He had gone through his roommate's pockets and found candy and some change.

Mary tapped him on the shoulder. John looked up at her, grinned, and shrugged as if to say, "OK, you caught me."

Mary often took John to the store. He took great pleasure in pushing the grocery cart down the aisles. He pushed while Mary steered. As an experiment, Mary put a small can of coffee in John's hand. Then she took it away and replaced it with a jar of instant coffee. She wanted to know if he knew the difference. As soon as he touched the instant coffee, he shook his head no. He preferred the real thing and did know the difference between the two containers.

After one of their shopping trips, Mary pulled her car into her driveway. Instead of getting out of the car, John indicated to Mary that he would like to sit in the driver's seat for a while.

"You drive?" Mary signed to him.

"Yes," John said.

Mary didn't think John could get in much trouble with the engine turned off, so she agreed to switch places.

John got behind the wheel, and Mary moved to the passenger seat. John grabbed the wheel and pretended to drive. His laughter filled the car as he pointed to his eyes, turned the wheel, and then smashed his fist into his hand to simulate an accident. He was having a wonderful time. Mary thought it was hilarious.

"There is no way on God's green earth," Mary said later as she told and retold the story, "that John is retarded. No possible way."

About a year after he arrived at the Haases, John's life changed dramatically again. Ken and Mary were splitting up. It happened quickly. Ken found someone else and told Mary that he was leaving. Twenty-five minutes later, Mary said, he walked out the door.

That night, when John, Mike, and Bill had gone to bed, Mary had time to think about what was happening. The day had started out normally, but by nightfall, her marriage was over, and she was going to lose her job. Springfield ARC's regulations said that only a married couple could run a group home. She had notified ARC immediately when Ken left. Mary knew she soon would have to leave as well.

For her, it was like divorcing and losing her children in the space of a few weeks. She was close to all three clients in her home, but especially to John. Maybe, she thought, it was because he needed her the most.

For the next few days, she made an effort to let John, Mike, and Bill think that everything was fine. And then, when another couple had been found to take over the group home, she told them that Ken wasn't coming back.

"Why?" John asked.

"He's just going to live somewhere else," Mary said.

"OK," John said, and he did not mention it again. His matter-of-fact response awakened Mary to the realization that John had seen so many people come and go in and out of his life, including his real family, wherever they were, that he was numb to it by now. She thought that he almost expected it. John still saw Ken on weekdays at the Bowden Center, so Mary thought that it might not seem much different to him.

Mary was allowed to stay in the group home for another month, while she searched for a new job and a place to live. Her parents and her sister were all houseparents for ARC group homes, so when she needed help, they came.

Mary left on 31 May 1984. That morning, John, Mike, and Bill were getting ready to go to Bowden. Mike and Bill knew that Mary was leaving that day because they had seen her packing. But John, as far as she knew, didn't know.

John came downstairs for breakfast. It was time to tell him. She let John touch her suitcase, just as she had seen Peter Krienbihl from the Helen Keller Center do a year earlier. She took his hand and signed to him that she was leaving.

A puzzled look came over John's face. He pointed to himself. "Am I leaving?" She said, "No," took his hand, and pointed it to herself. When John realized that it was Mary who was leaving, he stood still for a few moments while the bad news took hold. Then he began to cry. It was the only time Mary had ever seen him in tears.

He pointed at himself, then the door. "I am coming, too."

Mary, also in tears, took his hands in hers and said, "No." She put his hand on Mike. "You stay with Mike." Remembering that Mike would still be there seemed to make John feel better. Mike put his arm around John.

John signed to Mary, "I love you." With her tears wetting her face, Mary signed back, "I love you, too." And she walked out the door.

Groups

The new houseparents, a couple in their twenties, took over the group home after Mary left. She was asked by ARC to stay away from the house so that John and the others could adjust to the new houseparents. John had an especially difficult time with the transition. He had no rapport with the new couple.

Mary went by the house a couple of times without letting anyone know she was there. She saw John sitting in the porch swing. She thought he looked sad and diminished.

"There's something going out of him," Mary told her mother. "I can see it."

Perhaps John never really got used to losing the people who were close to him. Perhaps his age was catching up with him. If the Jacksonville authorities had been close with the estimate of 1929, he was in his midfifties when Mary left. If the ophthalmologist was right, he may have been in his early seventies. However old he was, a bit of the spirit that had enabled John to overcome so much and survive for so long died the day Mary left.

Mary met John again at a store about a year later. She walked up to him and touched him softly to let him know that someone was there. John turned and put his hand on her cheek to see if he recognized her. He moved his hand around her face and to her earlobe. He took the lobe in two fingers and studied it. There was something about the face, or maybe the ear, that was like a fingerprint to him. No two people's faces felt the same to him. Yes, he knew her, and he smiled.

"Can I have a hug?" she signed to him. He nodded, and they hugged for the last time.

By 1986 John, Mike, and Bill had all been transferred to a different ARC group home on the west side of Springfield. There were about eight other ARC clients in the home with John. He had a room to himself in the basement but shared his bathroom with the other clients who lived downstairs. John was still attending the Bowden Adult Center with Mike every day.

Terry and Janet Borkgren were John's group home houseparents. Janet had twenty-seven years of nursing experience, although none of it with a deaf, blind, and nonverbal man. In fact, she didn't know one of the residents was blind, deaf, and mute until she and her husband became managers of the group home. She was about to receive her on-the-job training.

The first time Janet saw John, he was downstairs in the TV room. When they met, John touched her face and head. Janet wore her hair curled tightly and very short. As soon as John felt that tightly curled hair, he had the mark he needed to always be able to identify her.

In the mornings, when the bus came to pick John up for the Bowden Center, John walked to it by himself. He could feel the pavement of the driveway under his shoes, and he simply followed it to the curb where the bus was waiting.

Since Janet didn't know hand-on-hand signing, she and John communicated through basic gestures. John started teaching her the gestures and signs he used. She learned first his signs for "bathroom," "drink," and "eat."

When Janet was a girl, her deaf uncle lived with her family. She learned how to communicate with him and watched how he acted and reacted. Those girlhood lessons served her well when she took over John's care.

She was impressed that John could do as much for himself as he could. She saw that he had his clothes sorted by color. Evidently, she thought, he could tell the colors by the touch and texture of the clothes. However he did it, he never mismatched his clothes, which he always picked out on his own.

Janet noticed that whenever one of the other clients in the home became agitated, John picked up on it. If someone was upset and punched a wall, or if someone stumbled and fell, John sensed it and either walked away from trouble or quickly put his hands up to protect himself in case someone was going to hit him.

The Borkgrens made it a point to get John out of the house. They took him to the movies or to church with them. John sat quietly throughout a movie, though he could only feel the vibrations of the sound. He also sat quietly in church, though he couldn't hear the sermon or the singing.

Clients in group homes in Springfield's ARC system were required to sign for their SSI checks. John made an *X*, which served as his signature for his checks. The Borkgrens co-signed with him. But, on occasion, when prompted to sign his name by one of the ARC assistants living in the house, John signed a name the Borkgrens thought was "Lewis."

Janet tried to ask him where the name "Lewis" came from. But she could not understand John's response, which was done hand-on-hand.

Meals at the group home were served family style, with large bowls of food placed on the table. Residents passed the bowls around the table. When the food reached John, someone took his hand and put it on the bowl so that he knew it was coming. He took the food and served himself. When his plate was full, he put his hand on the top of his plate. He then went in a clockwise direction, putting a finger into his food to get its location. When he had each portion of the meal located, he cut his meat and put gravy on his potatoes and salt and pepper where he wanted them. If he wanted water, he took a glass and went to the sink. He put one finger in his glass and turned on the water. When the water touched his finger, he knew his glass was full. After the meal was finished, his job was to help load the dishwasher.

For the third time since John left Lincoln, he was taught how to identify money. It seemed that each time he moved, he lost some of the skills that he must have identified only with a particular place. The Borkgrens helped him relearn the differences between coins, just as Mary Ransdell had at Jacksonville and the staff of the Helen Keller Center had in New York.

There must have been something of his old lessons that stayed with him. This time, he learned to differentiate between money values very quickly. In fact, Janet was convinced that John could tell the difference between a one-dollar bill and a five-dollar bill, though she never could figure out how he did it.

If John had any trouble relearning how to identify money, he had no trouble remembering how to hoard it. He found a secret hiding place for it and his other "valuables" that he picked up as he wandered around the house. He peeled back the lining on the underside of his mattress and slid a box of his things inside. But, for some reason, his box eventually was missing. When he discovered that it was gone, John shouted and waved his arms excitedly until someone came to see what was wrong. Whoever had taken the box, probably as a joke, quickly returned it.

At restaurants, the Borkgrens ordered for John. They could not communicate with him well enough yet for him to tell them what he wanted.

Janet soon learned of John's love of music, and they danced around the house in a two-step and a shuffle. There was usually music on while they danced, but John didn't always need it. If someone approached him and made a circle in his hand (a sign for "dance"), he would dance whether he felt vibrations from a stereo or not. One of the other residents had a harmonica, and one day, John picked it up and blew into it while doing a march step as if he were in a parade.

When John came out of his bedroom, he walked down a short hall, then turned left, right, and left again, until he reached the couch in the downstairs TV room. The Borkgrens' baby granddaughter sometimes sat in a playpen near the couch. As he entered the room, John usually felt inside the playpen to see if the baby was there. If she was, he always asked to hold her. He was so gentle with her that the Borkgrens had no qualms about letting him hold their granddaughter. When the baby wasn't there, John usually made some sounds and mimicked the rocking of the baby, just as Mary Ransdell had taught him to do.

The Fifth Farewell

Bill Corrington was one of the program technicians taking care of the residents at the group home. He helped the Borkgrens decipher the meanings of John's signs and gestures.

Bill worked various jobs at the group home, including staying awake through the night to clean the house and watch over the residents. One of the first things he learned about John was that John had a special chair. He learned that information the hard way—by moving the chair in order to clean under it. When John didn't find his chair exactly where it was supposed to be, he had a tantrum. Bill never moved it again without putting it back in its spot.

When Bill cleaned the top of John's dresser, he was careful to put every item back in its exact position. John's comb, toothbrush, and other items were arranged the same way every day so that John could find them.

While that was understandable, some of John's habits weren't as easily figured out. In the morning, as John got dressed, he performed an unusual ritual with his socks. When he pulled them on, he felt for the small, colored strip of fabric across their toes. Once he found it, he felt along that strip of stitching. He continued to pull on it, then feel it, until the strip of cloth was exactly straight across his toes. Only then would he put on his shoes. Perhaps aligning that stitching on his sock was one of the few things in his life that gave him a sense of control.

Bill, like the Borkgrens, did not want to let John sit and do nothing. He was determined to find activities that John could do. He put John at a table with a jigsaw puzzle that, when put together, made up a map of the United States. They worked on the puzzle with Bill guiding John's hands to the various pieces. John felt the shapes, then the shapes on the board, and worked at fitting them together. If he got one piece into its proper place, he and Bill regarded it as a good day's work.

John liked the game of fitting the puzzle together. He still had good manual dexterity, despite the thickening of the skin on his fingers, a side effect of his diabetes medicine. After several months of work on the puzzle, John was able to put all of the states in their proper places.

When the weather was good, the other residents at the group home played football or soccer outside. At first, John sat while the others played, or he walked short distances across the grass by himself. But Bill eventually drew him into the games. When he felt the soccer ball at his feet, he kicked it. Then he laughed.

There was a bicycle at the home, and Bill thought it would be a good idea to give John a ride. Bill helped John get on the saddle, then put John's feet on the pedals and his hands on the handlebars. Bill held onto John and pushed him slowly along the grass on the bike. John's face broke into a huge grin, and his feet tried to keep up with the pedals. When John seemed comfortable, Bill let go of the handlebars and let John steer as Bill held the bike upright and pushed. Soon, Bill held the bike with one arm instead of two. About thirty minutes after John had first climbed onto the bike, he was riding it slowly in the grass with Bill guiding him only slightly. John was as excited as a six year old with his first trainer. The other men at the group home heard the sound of John's laughter and came to watch him ride shakily around the yard. The commotion brought the Borkgrens out of the house as well. Under Bill's guidance, John learned to kick a football and to throw a softball. Back in Jacksonville, John and Mary Ransdell had rolled a ball between them as they sat on the floor, but John hadn't thrown a ball for any distance. He had seen it done in Lincoln, so he knew what Bill was trying to teach him.

Bill laid a stick on the ground and walked John up to it. When John's foot touched the stick, Bill stopped him. Gradually, he made John understand that he couldn't go beyond the stick. Then he gave John the ball and put him a few steps behind the stick. He showed John that he could take two or three steps to build up momentum, then throw the ball. At first, John could get it only a few inches in front of the stick. But the more they practiced, the better John became. Soon, whenever John was outside, he wanted to practice his throwing. He attracted attention by making noise, then doing a throwing motion. If Bill wasn't around, someone else helped John throw.

He was eventually entered in the softball throw event of the 1986 Special Olympics contest in Springfield. Nobody was sure which age group John belonged in, but they felt confident putting him in the fifty-and-over group.

At the meet, John threw the softball eleven meters and eleven centimeters, good for fourth place in his age group. He was given a ribbon in honor of his accomplishment. Back at the group home, everyone made a fuss over the ribbon. John sat on the couch for the rest of the day, bursting with pride. When he sensed someone had come into the room, he called out to get his or her attention and held the ribbon up to be seen. Even if it was someone who had seen it ten times already, he or she made sure to pat him on the shoulder.

In John's life, he had accomplished many things of importance, from learning how to go to the bathroom independently, to doing his own laundry. But he had never been given a ribbon for doing his laundry. After showing off his Special Olympics ribbon to the others in the group home, he kept it hidden in his box of valuables under the mattress.

John was never late for breakfast. After he was awakened, whoever woke him up, usually Bill Corrington, knew he could leave John alone while he helped the less independent residents. John would always get himself ready and come upstairs to the kitchen on time. So it was unusual on a March morning in 1987 when John didn't appear for breakfast. Bill told Janet that he had seen John out of bed and dressed, so he should have been at the table. But when Janet went downstairs to check on John, she found him back in his bed with his clothes on.

Janet took John's hand and gave him the sign for "eat." John shook his head. She drew a question mark in his hand. He pointed to his leg. Janet took his arm and tried to get him up, but John shouted, "Aaaaaah!" and pulled his arm away.

Janet went back upstairs to get Bill. "I need you to go downstairs and help me with John," she told him. They went to John's room, and Janet made John understand that they wanted to know where he was hurting. He pointed to his foot. Janet removed his shoes and socks and saw that his foot was swollen and cold. She tried to get a pulse in his foot but couldn't.

"I'm going to have to call the doctor," she told Bill. "I think we've got something serious going on here."

Janet and Bill took John to see a doctor that morning. John had been treated for a gastric ulcer the year before, but only on an outpatient basis. As she got ready to leave, Janet wasn't at all sure how John would respond should he have to be hospitalized.

John would not take Janet's arm for support as they left the house, so she placed his hands on the backs of her shoulders, and John followed her out of the house, limping as he walked. The doctor who examined him diagnosed a blood clot in John's leg and admitted him to the hospital right away. John underwent surgery to remove the clot on 17 March 1987.

Janet told the nurses that in order to communicate with John, they should find someone who could do hand-on-hand signing. But there was no one available. Even if there had been, it wouldn't have done them much good. It took time to learn which gestures and signs John understood. It took more time to learn his unique way of communicating.

Generally, if John was prepared in advance for any touching of his body by a nurse or doctor, he was cooperative. But the fact that the nurses couldn't communicate with John after his surgery meant that he was unprepared for whatever they wanted to do with him. He resisted the nurses, some-times physically, when they attempted to take care of him. He had no way of knowing whether the person touching him wanted to help him or whether he or she wanted to take something from him. As long as he didn't know, he was defensive.

Then, the second day after John's surgery, Janet went to visit him. He wasn't in his room. Janet inquired about that and was told that John had been moved to another room. Janet found him disoriented and confused by the change of rooms. When she returned the next day, they had moved him to yet another room.

The nurses told Janet they couldn't understand why John was so upset and uncooperative. They told her that, several times each night, John woke up screaming. Janet was furious over the constant moving of John. Perhaps he was hard to handle, Janet told the nurses, but if given enough time to get to know them and his room, she was sure he would improve.

"You can't keep moving him," Janet told the head nurse on John's floor. "You are getting this man so disoriented he can't find his way to the bathroom. He can function on his own. He can dress himself, feed himself, and he can walk to the bathroom if he knows where it's at. You can't continually change the orientation for a blind person. He'll be lost."

After that, the hospital staff left John in the same room. That helped calm him, but physically he continued to decline. The doctors believed he may have suffered another stroke. John could no longer feed himself or dress himself. He could barely walk.

John was released to Janet's care on 30 March. She believed that he would do much better once he returned to the familiarity of his home. She wanted to move his bedroom to the main floor so that he wouldn't have to negotiate the stairs. But John refused any efforts to move him from his basement room. His room was his room, and that was the only one he wanted. After all of the changes, turmoil, and moving he had already done, he clung desperately now to whatever stability he had. To appease him, the Borkgrens let him stay downstairs.

But even though he was back in his old room, he couldn't regain his bearings. He was still virtually helpless. It was as if the twenty years of learning and struggle that he had undergone in Jacksonville, New York, and Springfield had never happened. He needed help with even the smallest of tasks. He showed no desire to regain his independence. Then, one morning, he went into a seizure. It was more than Janet could handle.

According to the Springfield Aid to Retarded Citizens regulations, a group home resident was required to be at least partially independent. The homes were not set up or staffed adequately for someone who needed constant care. There were five other men living in the home. The Borkgrens couldn't spend all their time with John. Janet and the ARC staff reluctantly decided that John should be moved to a place where he could get the help he needed.

After a search of area nursing homes and contacting groups established to help the retarded, John was accepted by Peoria Aid for Retarded Citizens, which promised to find a suitable place for him to live.

John and Barbara Smiley never met, but when John was accepted by Peoria Aid for Retarded Citizens, it was the second time that Barbara's influence had a profound effect on John's life. The first was when she chaired the Commission on Mental Retardation. Its findings eventually resulted in John being moved out of Lincoln to Jacksonville.

In 1957, about the time Barbara was picked to chair Governor Stratton's commission, Peoria Aid for Retarded Children was founded. That group was guided by a board, the membership of which included Barbara. She became executive director of the organization in 1959. Its scope was then widened beyond assisting children exclusively. To suit its new role, the group's name eventually changed to "Peoria Aid for Retarded Citizens" (PARC).

In 1974, the Illinois Department of Mental Health was reorganized. In the reshuffle, Barbara left PARC and took a job with the new department as coordinator of a twenty-six-county region served by the department. She helped arrange placement for the retarded who had no place to live in their own community.

Before leaving PARC, Barbara wrote a federal grant application that was approved, funded, and led to the construction of the Peoria Retarded Adult Center, which opened in 1972. Its purpose was to provide living space and training for fifty-two retarded adults who were too advanced to live in a state institution. The name of the Peoria Retarded Adult Center was eventually changed to the "Smiley Living Center." It was done to honor Barbara's decades of work on behalf of retarded children and adults—work that began after a doctor's recommendation that Barbara and Karl's daughter be sent to an institution and forgotten. In Peoria, John's home was going to be the Smiley Living Center.

John was told he would be leaving the Borkgrens' group home in Springfield. Janet took his hands and made a sign for "house." She was trying to tell John he was going to a new house, but she didn't know whether he understood. Whether he did or he didn't, he showed no reluctance to leave. In his present state, he would go wherever Janet took him.

There was no excitement when he left. There were no tears as there had been when Mary Haas left his first group home. Either he had become numbed to being sent from one place to another, or he was too ill to care about anything.

On 23 April 1987, six weeks after his blood clot surgery, John was taken to a PARC-operated respite care center. The care center was created to be a place where parents could leave their retarded children in case of an emergency or if they needed a break. Parents could put their children there for a maximum of thirty days a year. Now, it was where John would stay until PARC therapists could design a care program for him.

As she prepared to say goodbye to John, Janet told a care center staff member, "If he gets better, we'd like to have him back." She knew that would never happen, but it made her feel better to tell someone that she liked John and would take him in again if she could. Janet and John shared a quick hug, and then she, too, was gone from his life.

7 Unknown, Unmarked: Peoria, 1987–1993

We respected the way he lived his life, considering all his disabilities. He was still his own person. He did things on his terms. Most people with those disabilities would just be sitting in a corner someplace.
—Kim Cornwell, Peoria Aid to Retarded Citizens

Barbara Smiley's Other Baby

John stayed at the PARC respite care center just over a month. That was enough time for him to recover physically from his surgery. And it was enough time for him to become oriented to his new surroundings. By the end of his stay at his temporary home, he was much improved.

On 8 June 1987, John walked through the doors of the Smiley Living Center. Its staff members, like the staff of Springfield's ARC, called John "John Doe Boyd," though they never knew where the "Boyd" came from. They thought that it must have come from records that listed him as "John Doe, boy." Someone, they assumed, just added a *d*. They used the name "John Boyd" for the same reason Springfield's ARC had—it made John seem more like a person than an anonymous client.

The Smiley Center must have felt familiar to John. It had the same feel and the same smells as the Jacksonville Developmental Center and the Helen Keller Center. He must have known immediately that he was back in some kind of institution. He felt the hard linoleum under his shoes and the steel rails along the walls. He sensed a large group of residents milling around in the common recreation room inside the front door.

After four years of living in private homes with only a few other people, coming to Smiley was probably a shock. It may have been depressing for John to realize that he was back in such a place, though Smiley was a universe away from the horrors of Lincoln.

John was put in the care of Eric Sutter, and Eric wasn't at all sure he was up to the job. He had never worked with anyone who was deaf, blind, and couldn't speak. In fact, no one on the Smiley staff had. Eric admitted that John scared him. John, in turn, sensed that he had the upper hand with Eric.

"I can't communicate with him," Eric complained. "How am I supposed to talk to him? I've never worked in this field before. I don't know what to do."

When it was time for John's shower or bath, Eric's job was to make sure John got undressed, went into the tub, and cleaned up. But when Eric started to help John into the bath, John shouted, "Noooooo," and waved him away. This, Eric thought, was going to be a challenge.

Most of the Smiley staff members regarded John as a challenge. Since he was their first deaf-blind-mute resident, the techniques they had been taught for communicating with the deaf were useless. They had to resort to unorthodox methods until a communication system could be worked out.

The first time the fire alarm went off after John arrived, everyone headed for the doors. They knew the drill, but John did not. Eric grabbed John's arm to lead him quickly out the door, but John, not knowing what was happening, pulled his arm away and refused to go anywhere.

"Oh, Lord," Eric thought. "How am I going to do this? How can I make him understand a fire drill?"

Eric nudged John, hoping he would move. John became angry. "Uuuuhh yuh, yuh, yuh, yuh, yuh," he said loudly and waved his arms, almost hitting Eric in the face. Eric nudged John again, but that only made John angrier. The fire drill went on without John. If it had been a real fire, he would have been a cinder.

It took John a few weeks, but he eventually learned the universal sign for "fire drill." Eric was able to teach him that whenever someone drew a large X on his back with his or her fingers, that meant he was to go out of the building.

Now it was the Smiley staff's turn to learn how John communicated. At each stage of his life, from the moment he was found in Jacksonville, the process was repeated. The only people who never learned it were the police officers who found him. They, of course, weren't around him long enough to learn what he was trying to say. He started from scratch in Lincoln, Jacksonville, New York, Springfield, and, now, Peoria. When John arrived at the Smiley Center, the only sign he made that was understood immediately was "bathroom."

John liked peanuts. The normal sign for "peanuts" is to click a thumbnail out from a front tooth. But John's sign was to make believe he was cracking open a shell. People eventually understood what he meant.

Most of the time, communicating with John was like playing charades. Understanding him was a matter of deciphering his pantomimes. Some of his signs were close to American Sign Language but always just a little off. The Smiley staff knew that the ASL sign for "candy" was putting the knuckle of a forefinger into the cheek. But for "candy," John pinched his cheek with his thumb and forefinger and made a sucking sound. His meaning was clear, even though it wasn't the textbook way of doing it.

John could generally understand the sign for any word if it was "modeled" for him. That is, if someone could describe a house with her hands as John felt them, then he knew what she was talking about. That was the advantage of having sight until he was in his forties.

Steve Roth was one of several PARC staffers who eventually took John to the doctor. Steve created his own way of letting John know when it was time to go. Instead of signing into John's hand, "It is time to get in the car and go to the doctor," Steve took John's hands and pointed them at John ("you"), then he pointed John's hands at himself ("me"), and then Steve moved John's hands up and down as if he were driving a car ("go in the car"). And John knew that he was to go with Steve in the car. And John also knew that, more often than not, a trip in the car meant going to the doctor.

In every new place John lived, history repeated itself. The Smiley staff was sure that John was more advanced than the notation of "severely retarded" still in his records indicated. The Smiley staff also came to the same conclusion that had been reached at every other institution in which John had lived: "John really doesn't belong here."

He Wrote "Lewis"

Ever since he had lost his sight, John had the ability to "see" with his hands. Whether it was recognizing people by their faces, hair, or earlobes or finding his way around a room, he had been able to rely on his sense of touch.

But in Peoria his tactile sense was not as sharp. Part of his decline was due to the ravages of time. John was approaching sixty years of age at least, and his senses weren't as sharp as they once were. Also, the diabetes medication he'd been taking for twenty years had dried his skin so badly that it blistered and thickened. His sense of touch had dulled to the point where he could no longer identify people by merely touching their earlobes or a part of their face. His hands lingered over their faces and hair now, and still he had trouble finding something by which to identify them.

He eventually learned the faces of the people who cared for him most often. He laughed or smiled when he recognized them. Tom Cubr, a communication instructor, worked with John on hand-on-hand signing. Whenever Tom arrived, John reached out to touch his face. He knew Tom by his beard. Whenever John felt the beard, he laughed, and that made Tom laugh.

John had been living at Smiley for more than two years when he was visited by Bob Griffiths, a case worker for the Illinois Department of Rehabilitation Services. Bob was there to observe how well, or how poorly, John was doing with his basic living skills. The first time Bob saw him, John was strumming a guitar. Instead of approaching him immediately, Bob stood back and watched. As he did, John put down the guitar but picked up a harmonica and blew into it.

Bob finally walked gingerly over to John and touched him to indicate that he was there. Using hand-on-hand signs, Bob tried a couple of greetings. John didn't know who this person was or what he wanted, and, besides, he was much more interested in playing music. He virtually ignored Bob, but Bob was content to observe John from a distance.

As he watched John play the instruments, Bob instinctively knew three things about John: John was not severely retarded; he had not been blind all his life; and he probably had some sense of hearing, no matter how slight.

Bob, who was deaf, also had years of experience in working with the deaf and blind. He knew that if they didn't have the usual "blindisms" (rhythmic moving of the head, for example), they had not been blind since birth. He had already read John's records. As he watched him, the "severely retarded" evaluation he had seen came to mind. But Bob knew, from the way John handled the guitar and harmonica, that the evaluation was wrong. Bob thought John was able to hear some type of sound from the instruments by the way John moved and by his efforts to make music.

In a follow-up report after his visit with John, Bob told his supervisors that John probably had good communication skills at one time, but it was likely that he had lost them during his long years of institutionalization.

"People like John may have done well at twenty-one or twenty-two years old," he told them, "but when they lose that home environment and go into an institution, they decline. Forty years later, I come along, and they're like vegetables when it comes to communicating."

The Smiley staff tried to explain to John that he could choose how he would spend his days. Because John was nearing sixty, he qualified for PARC's older adults program, which is geared toward giving its participants more leisure time. Or he could choose to have a job in a Peoria workshop that hired the mentally disabled to perform unskilled labor for local companies. He told them he would prefer the workshop. At first, workshop jobs were brought to John at the Smiley Center.

"He can do just about anything," Terri Ingles, John's case manager at Smiley, told the people at the workshop. "All you have to do is show him once, and he's got it."

Soon, the staff decided that John was ready to go to the PARC workshop. Each weekday morning, John was escorted from the front door of the Smiley Center to a city bus for his trip. A bus monitor usually came along to make sure nothing happened on the way. The staff members had learned from trips John had taken in their vans that he had the dangerous habit of undoing his seat belt and walking around while the van was moving.

At the end of his ride, John was escorted off the bus and to the workshop door. It must have reminded John of Mike and the way he led him to the Bowden Adult Center back in Springfield. The familiarity of it and the good memories of his experiences with Mike and Bowden probably made it easier for John to adjust to the new routine in Peoria.

Smiley residents, like John, who earned money from working had it deposited in a house account along with their government support. Whenever John wanted to withdraw money from his account, he was required to sign his name. This was explained to him using hand-on-hand sign language. The first time someone put a cash withdrawal form in front of John and handed him a pen, he wrote a name that the staff determined to be "Lewis." The name was written in cursive lettering, not printed.

The Smiley staff members didn't know that John had ever signed the same name for the Borkgrens in Springfield. Nonetheless, they came to the same conclusion that the Borkgrens had, that the name he signed was "Lewis."

The story about John printing the name "Lewis" quickly spread through the staff. Staffers regarded it as a clue to his identity. They wanted to learn more about him—they were about to.

John sat in the common living area at Smiley, and its life went on as usual around him. He had been in Smiley for over two years. As always, there were many other residents sitting near him and walking by him. The staff was busy attending to first one person and then another.

John stood up and for the first time at Smiley began to act out a story. As the staff and other residents watched him, John acted out a parade. He portrayed different animals by using his hands and arms. He also pretended to be playing a horn in a band. In his mind, he was someplace far from Peoria, watching a parade go by.

John put his arms in front of himself, pointed them down, and swung them—the elephant. If Ken and Mary Haas had been there, they could have told the Smiley staff that this was all very familiar to them. They could have told how, once John got to know them, the same stories had come tumbling out of him. But that, as John always signed, was "long ago."

Staff members from all around the living area stopped to watch John as he "told" his story. They gave each other looks as if to say, "Do you see what I'm seeing?"

A few days later, it happened again. This time, John was at the dinner table. He put down his knife and fork and made it known that he wanted everyone's attention by bellowing loudly and waving his arms. He acted out another story. This time, he was driving. He waved to the left and then to the right. He reached over his head and pulled on a cord to make the horn blow. When he did that, the staff knew that John was driving a semitruck. If he had been pretending to be in a car, the horn would have been on the steering wheel.

John performed his stories frequently enough that they were no longer a surprise. One day, he was riding a horse. He made the motion of cracking a whip, complete with clicking sounds with his tongue. To those who watched him, it seemed that he was portraying a ringmaster in a circus.

The staff members who had seen John act out his stories talked among themselves about the things they had seen him do and what they could mean. Was he, they wondered, trying to tell them something about his life? When had he ever gone drinking? Yet, there he was a few days later, pantomiming the story of a wild night on the town. The staff wondered, exactly as the Haases had, whether John's parents owned a tavern when he was a child, and he was remembering it now. His pantomimed stories added to the mystery of who he was and fueled the Smiley staff's desire to find out.

The staffers began to regard him as something more than their first deaf-blind-mute client. The early awkwardness between them was gone. Their relationship had progressed beyond the early goals of just learning how to communicate. Things had evolved (maybe it was the first time they saw him write "Lewis") into something more. John was not just a deaf-blind-mute man anymore. He had his own identity, even if no one knew his real name.

John walked with a dignity and pride the staff didn't often see in the other residents. As Bob Griffiths observed, John's head didn't droop. He had no rhythmic swaying of his body or head. He didn't frequently put a knuckle to his eye the way many people who are blind do. This all served to elevate him in the staff's collective mind; it put him a cut above the others.

The Smiley staff members had no idea that John had ever been able to see. They were never given that information. It might have explained where he had seen the parades and the circuses—on TV or in one of the movies he had seen regularly in Lincoln.

John became accomplished at getting the Smiley staff members, especially the young and inexperienced among them, to do whatever he wanted them to do. They lit his cigarettes for him, brought him peanuts, gave him extra food or his favorite "collectibles," including the coins that he still loved to hoard.

There was a soda machine just off the main living area of Smiley. It became John's favorite place to sit. He propped his feet up on the machine and sat there for hours, sometimes sleeping and sometimes humming to himself. Frequently, he leaned forward and checked the soda machine coin return. He found change in it often enough to keep him coming back. He could sense the vibrations when someone used the machine. As soon as they walked away, he was at the coin return.

He was sitting at the soda machine when his old friend Bill Corrington, the man who had taught John to throw a softball and ride a bike back in Springfield, came to visit him.

It had been about five years since Bill had last seen John. After gently letting John know he was there, Bill took John's hand and started leading him to a sofa, so they could sit down. But John stopped, not knowing who this was or where he was taking him. He reached out to feel Bill's face and head. As soon as he felt the bald spot on the back of Bill's head, there was a spark of recognition. Then Bill took John's hands, placed them on his hips, and started to dance. John laughed. He knew now who he was with. To prove it, John pretended to kick a football and ride a bike the way they had done back at the group home.

Bill showed the Smiley staff how John had danced back at the group home. He led John to a piano, put John's hands on it, and John eagerly pounded the keys.

About an hour after Bill arrived, he signed to John that he had to leave. John became upset, shouted, "Ooooo," and shook his head. Bill left John that day just as he had found him, sitting at the soda machine waiting for someone to forget his change.

At Smiley, John took his "pack rat" behavior to new heights. He strapped belts to himself under his clothes, then fastened small bags to the belts. In the bags, he put his coins, scraps of paper, small packages of sugar and coffee sweetener, toothbrushes, combs, paper clips—whatever he could find and claim for his own. The staff was concerned that John would strap the belts around himself so tightly that they would cut off his circulation.

John eventually found something he preferred over the belts and pouches he had strapped across his body. It was an old shaving kit bag. He put a string through one of its straps and tied the string into a loop big enough to go around his neck. Then he carefully wrapped his treasures in plastic and put them inside the bag.

When he had everything arranged just as he wanted it, he hung the shaving bag from his neck under his shirt. He didn't like to take a shower anymore when he knew other people would be around. He was afraid someone would steal his shaving bag.

He was more obsessed than ever with finding things. He walked along couches, feeling under the cushions in search of loose change. He crawled on the floor, pulling the screens from the air vents and feeling inside for whatever he could find. Smiley maintenance workers complained about John dismantling the air vents. John was told to leave the vents alone. When he didn't, he was usually scolded. But it did little good.

Whenever John went to a doctor's office, he checked the couch and chair cushions for change. When he could, he took the cushions and threw them on the floor to make his search easier. It was inevitable that he would touch someone who was sitting on the couch or chair. When he did, he usually bellowed angrily and walked away.

The staff members tried to break him of the scavenging habit. Whenever they caught him going through the sofa cushions, they tapped him on the arm or shoulder. When he knew he'd been caught, John was embarrassed and backed away as if to say, "You got me. I won't do it again." Either that, or he grew angry that he was caught. After he was stopped from scrounging, he would simply wait a while, then sweep his arms through the area surrounding him to make sure no one was there. If no one was, he resumed searching.

After being caught enough times, he learned to be more cagey about his "treasure hunting." He sat at his usual spot at the soda machine for a long time, and then, taking great care to be sneaky, he rose and worked his way along the wall. If he ran into a wheelchair, that was even better. He knew that people who used wheelchairs often had a backpack or bag in the back of the chair where they kept their things. Whenever John felt a wheelchair, he would immediately rifle the bag in the back and take whatever he found that interested him.

Usually around dinner time, John wound his way toward the food cart in the dining room. As he went, he trailed his hands along the windows and walls to keep his bearings. He tried to make it look as if he were simply strolling around the room, in case anyone was watching. But he had a purpose in mind. He wanted to steal food, small packets of coffee creamer, or any other items he could from the food cart.

Kim Cornwell, his case manager at Smiley, watched him go through this routine. She knew what John was going to do. Before he could reach the food cart, she caught up to him and signaled for him to take her arm and come with her. John felt her arm and hair. When he realized it was Kim, he said, "Whoooaaa!" and backed away. He would not follow her away from the cart. She took his hand and made a sign for what she thought was "follow." But rather than follow her, John began laughing boisterously. He pretended to take a drink from a bottle or can, then staggered around as if he were drunk.

Puzzled and amused, Kim turned to another staff member who was watching and said, "What did I do? Sign that we should go for a drink?"

Portraying drinking was a habit of John's. So was his imitation of performing on a piano. That led the staff to wonder again about the role a tavern might have played in John's early life.

No Prints

On 20 March 1990, John was taken to Robert Lewis, a Peoria psychologist. Lewis was asked to evaluate John's mental capacity so that the Smiley staff could plan a more effective therapy program for John. The evaluation took place in a private room near the main office of United Cerebral Palsy. Darrell Wilson of PARC went with him.

"He is bright," Wilson told Lewis. "He takes care of himself well. He dresses himself. He does all his own hygiene, shaves and shampoos his hair. He was found on the streets. He can survive on the streets." As Wilson and Lewis were talking, John got their attention and made the sign for "peanut." Darrell put his thumb in John's palm with his index finger turned upward, which John understood to mean "later."

Lewis and Wilson went back to their conversation, and John became increasingly bored. He stretched his arms to explore his surroundings in the interview room. Wilson gently stopped him, and John reacted angrily.

"He's looking for money," Wilson explained. "His only trouble at Smiley Living Center is his roaming around, looking for things. He's very cooperative, though. He doesn't tease or hit the others, but he has his refusal point. If he's pushed past that, he can get physical. For a guy who's blind and can't hear or talk, he's pretty bright."

Lewis concluded that there was no intelligence test he could give John that would produce anything valid. "[Based] on what I know of John, my estimate [for a mental age] is close to a six-year, zero months," Lewis reported. "This very approximate estimate, realizing clearly that it is purely this, computes to be an IQ of thirty-eight, which would place him in the range earlier described as 'moderate mental retardation.'

"His only measurable accomplishment was that when given a pencil by Darrell, he felt it carefully, then slowly wrote on a blank paper that I provided his only word ever drawn out: 'Lewis.' This almost illegible written word is assumed to be what was once his actual name. As we completed this assessment, and John was quietly sitting in a solid office chair with arms, I shook his hand in appreciation of his cooperation and tolerance. He responded warmly by feeling my hand. Then, releasing it, he felt my arm and then touched my head."

Back at Smiley, John was given another white cane to help him get around. But it became apparent after having the cane only a short time that he was using it as a weapon more than to help him navigate. He was walking with the cane when he came near another Smiley resident. The resident accidentally bumped into John. Immediately, John whirled around and whacked the other resident with his cane. After a couple of similar incidents, the cane was taken from John.

There were occasional fights among the residents of Smiley. There was nowhere near the violence John had experienced in Lincoln, but he was involved in a few encounters just the same.

John was caught once with his hands around another resident's throat. Nobody saw what had led up to John's attack. The staff members speculated that the other resident bumped into John or tried to take something from him, and John lost his temper.

Staff also noticed that John had stopped using the men's bathroom in a hall near the main living area. This, being out of the ordinary for John, caused some concern.

"John," one employee signed to him, "why are you not going in the bathroom?" In reply, John made a kicking motion and pointed to himself. The staff speculated from that response that someone had kicked John while he was using the bathroom, and he didn't want to risk more attacks by going there again. Despite the efforts of the staff to get him to do so, he still refused to use the bathroom, which raised another question. If he wasn't using the bathroom, what was he using?

The answer was discovered when an aide accidentally walked in on John in his room and caught him urinating in a paper cup. The aide, not sure

what to do, waited to see what would happen. John, unaware that anyone was nearby, finished and then felt along the wall until he came to the
window. He opened it and threw the cup of urine outside. Almost. Some
of it splashed onto the wall and floor.

The aide reported the incident to custodians, who came to John's room
to clean it. They moved a dresser aside and found that, apparently, this
had been going on for some time. The paint on the wall behind the dresser
had peeled from all of the urine spilled near the window.

As soon as John sensed that his dresser was being moved, he went into
a tirade. "Naaaahhhh, naaaaah!" he bellowed and moved menacingly toward the workers. He was stopped before he reached them, which made
him even more upset. The dresser turned out to be one of his favorite
hiding places for his treasures of coffee sweetener, paper towels, and peanuts. He was afraid the workers were going to steal some of his stash.

John eventually regained his composure. The custodians cleaned his
walls and carpet. The staff members concentrated on getting John to use
the bathroom again. They were only partially successful. He stopped
urinating in paper cups, but he went outside and relieved himself in the
grass instead.

From the day John had first written "Lewis" for them, the staff members
at Smiley became more intrigued with discovering his identity. They believed his pantomimes to be hints into his past. But the trail was almost
fifty years old. Learning anything about John's identity this far removed
from 1945 and a Jacksonville alley was almost impossible.

Each year, Peoria Aid for Retarded Citizens held a meeting to discuss
the situation of each of its clients. In 1990, one topic of John's evaluation
was his true identity. A suggestion was made that the best way to find out
who John was would be to get his fingerprints and send them to a law
enforcement agency. Perhaps the authorities could match him to someone reported missing in the 1940s. If that happened, John might even be
reunited with his family. The Smiley staff found it an exciting possibility.

Kevin Pilger of PARC called the Illinois State Police in January 1991.
He explained John's unusual situation and asked whether it would be possible for the state police to help with the fingerprint idea. The state police
agreed to help and sent a man to Smiley. He brought an ink pad and paper to take John's prints.

It was nearly impossible to make John understand what was going to
happen. Someone took John's hand and put it into the ink, but he pulled
away and shouted, "AAAAAAHHH!" They were finally able to press John's

fingers into the ink, but only because some people familiar to him were asking him to do it.

After examining the ink stains John had made, the investigator from the state police department had some bad news for the Smiley staff. Because of the long years of taking diabetes medication, John's fingers were so cracked and dry that no clear fingerprint could be found. It was only fitting. The man with no name had no fingerprints.

In July 1992, John began complaining of pain. His pantomiming stopped, and he went back to sitting quietly alone. All he wanted to do was sleep. He had always gone to bed early in the evening, but now he headed for bed at 6:00 or 6:30 P.M. And he resisted getting up in the morning.

John's urine was checked regularly as part of his treatment for diabetes. Employees noticed that he had blood in his urine, and he was scheduled to be examined by a doctor. The examination revealed that John had colon cancer.

He underwent surgery for a colon resection and was given a good prognosis. Other than losing some weight during his recovery, he didn't seem to be set back much by the operation. He went back to the workshop, and most of his old enthusiasm returned. His physical recovery was remarkably fast for someone who was very likely over sixty. His mind, however, was not as sharp as it had been.

Each year, an overall evaluation of John's progress was made. It took into effect a wide variety of categories, including his level of physical ability, his social and communication skills, and how well he could function on his own. By December 1992, John's evaluation showed him functioning in all ways at the level of a four-year-old.

The Smiley Center staff threw a party for the residents during special holidays. John had bobbed for apples at a Halloween party that fall as if he'd been doing it all his life. At Christmas, staff members bought presents for him. Because of his dancing and swaying to music, many of his presents were music related. One year, he received a guitar. He was very excited about it until he opened his next present. He felt it and smelled it until he was sure it was—candy. It immediately went inside his shirt, the most secure place he could think of to put it.

For Christmas 1992, the staff at Smiley gave John a harmonica. When he opened the box and pulled out the harmonica, he felt it until he recognized what it was. When he did, he smiled and put it to his mouth to blow through it. Nobody was sure he could hear any of the noise that came from the harmonica, but it became one of his most cherished possessions.

By the fall of 1993, John's health problems had returned. He had lost his ability to control his bladder. He complained constantly of various pains. He wasn't often in a good mood. The storytelling stopped again. He finally had to be rushed to an emergency room because of bleeding from his penis. In the hospital, it was learned that John's colon cancer had returned and spread.

John was given only a short time to live. After he was admitted to Proctor Hospital early in October, Smiley staff members brought him his money and the other things he kept in his shaving kit. But he refused to take them. These were his most precious possessions, the things he kept closest to him. They meant nothing to him now.

John was not told the seriousness of his condition. No one at the hospital knew how to communicate with him, and the staff at Smiley believed that he already knew. When John entered the hospital, someone from Smiley was by his side around the clock. He had no one else. The staffers knew that if they weren't there, John would be alone. Beyond that, they had, in the past six years, become fond of John. The Smiley staff members took turns sitting with him because they wanted to.

Whatever the nurses did, John tried his best to undo. He tried to take his urine catheter out and tried to pull IV needles from his arm. He was eventually put in restraints for his own protection.

Amy Stepe, one of the Smiley staffers, stayed with John most of the time. Whenever someone came to administer John's medicine or to examine him, Stepe warned John first. She let John feel the catheter or syringes and IV tubes before they were inserted. When he knew what was coming, it made all the difference for him.

John was returned to Smiley, but when he wouldn't eat and became dangerously dehydrated, he was sent back to the hospital. The Smiley Living Center didn't have the medical resources to care for someone who needed constant nursing. He would either have to stay in the hospital or be sent somewhere else. Arrangements were made for John to be sent to Peoria's Sharon Oaks Nursing Home, where its nurses could take care of him around the clock.

John was taken to Sharon Oaks in an ambulance in October 1993. They brought him in on a stretcher. John didn't know where he was.

Smiley's residents asked where John had gone. The staff told them that John was going to live somewhere else and wouldn't be coming back. Some of the residents were saddened to hear that John was not coming back. Some of them cried and told anyone who would listen that "John was my best friend." They did it even if they barely knew him. It was their way of getting attention or acting out their feelings of bewilderment and loss.

Those residents who said little or nothing about it had, like John, seen many people come and go from their lives. One more loss, one more person who suddenly disappeared, meant nothing.

The Last Farewell of John Doe No. 24

At Sharon Oaks, John was fed through a tube inserted in his stomach. He pulled the tube out several times. A doctor eventually ordered that John be given solid food since he wasn't going to keep the stomach tube in anyway.

The move to Sharon Oaks began the now-familiar orientation process once again for John. He seemed to be depressed that, as ill as he was, he had to start over in another new place with more new people to get to know. He was pleased when some of the familiar people from Smiley came to visit.

In his first few days at Sharon Oaks, whenever someone put John into a chair, he would attempt to stand and walk. But he was too weak to put one foot in front of the other.

If someone came to take his blood pressure and didn't let John feel the bulb and the inflatable arm wrap before beginning, he bolted upright in his bed and protested loudly. If he was allowed to touch the instruments first, he let them take his blood pressure with no resistance.

Whenever a doctor came to see him, someone would give him the sign for "doctor" on his wrist. That also seemed to help.

In November, his condition worsened. He lost control of his bowels and sometimes fouled his bed. When he did, he became distraught. He couldn't stand to be dirty. It must have reminded him of Lincoln.

By mid-November, he came to know one or two people on the Sharon Oaks staff. The solid food strengthened him, and John rallied. He had progressed enough to be taken out of his room in a wheelchair and into the recreation area. He occasionally felt well enough to take out his harmonica, blow a few notes, and make an effort to stand up and dance. The staff at Sharon Oaks was just beginning to learn what all of the others before them had learned—there was more to John than any of them thought. If things went as they always had, they would soon become intrigued by the mystery man with no name who had found his way to them.

Perhaps the desire to find out who he really was would be kindled in the staff at Sharon Oaks as it was with staffers before them. It was just a matter of time before it all repeated itself.

By 28 November, John had been at Sharon Oaks for a month. That morning, he was pushed in a wheelchair into the dining room for breakfast. He ate eggs and cold cereal; drank a glass of fruit juice; and, still his favorite, drank a cup of coffee. An aide took him back to his room after the meal to make sure that John was clean and dry. He was then brought back to the recreation area.

Someone handed John a game. It was a board with holes of different shapes and sizes and pegs that matched the shapes. By feeling the pegs and the holes, he was supposed to match them. His tactile senses weren't sharp enough anymore for him to finish the game. He simply toyed with the different pieces.

John sat quietly in a morning sun that he could not see, alone with his thoughts. Perhaps his thoughts drifted back to another fall, just like this one, when the bright lights of a Jacksonville police car lit up the night in the alley where he was scrounging for food. Maybe he remembered sliding into the squad car to begin a journey from which he would never return.

He sat alone, inside a shell that few people had ever penetrated. He may have remembered the smell of cattle on another fall day. He may have recalled how he walked out the door of his farm and into the free night air. He could almost feel the water of Salt Creek on his feet and the sweet taste of freedom—the only freedom he had ever known—on his tongue.

His thoughts may have wandered through his past to the soft kindness of a woman as she took his hand and signed, "Good job," to him. He raised his head at that memory as he thought he smelled Mary Ransdell's Shalimar perfume.

He may have thought that it had been so long since he held a baby in his arms. If, just at that moment, someone had glanced at the old man in his wheelchair, she might have seen him pretend to cradle Terry Malone's baby in his arms once more and rock it back and forth.

In those last few minutes before he slumped over, dying in his wheel-chair, did his thoughts turn to his old Lincoln friend Albert, to a fight, to a summer festival, or perhaps to the hug Mary Haas gave him as she said goodbye?

John was rushed to his room. Someone administered CPR. An ambulance was on its way. A nurse, Donna Romine, was with John in his room as they worked on him. She said later that when John's time came, he left the world as suddenly and as mysteriously as he had appeared in it. No one knows for sure what killed John—it could have been the cancer, a stroke, or a massive heart attack. There was no one to request an autopsy.

John's body was taken to the Simons Mortuary in Peoria. He didn't own a suit he could be buried in, but Simons kept a few suits on hand for just such an emergency. Even though there would be no wake with an open casket, John was laid out in a suit and a tie. No one but a few of the funeral home employees saw him before the lid of the casket was closed. Just before it was, Mary Wilkerson of Simons added a final, extra touch. She unbuttoned John's suit coat, clipped off the end of his tie with a scissors, and stuck the piece into the breast pocket of his suit to give him a pocket stuffer to match his tie. Then she buttoned his suit coat again, and the casket was closed.

There were no funeral services, only a few words said at John's graveside. He was taken to Parkview Cemetery to be buried in a plot for hardship cases that was owned by the Salvation Army.

One of the funeral home's drivers, Wayne Jordan, was called on to conduct John's graveside service. Jordan was studying to become a minister, and since John didn't have a regular clergyman to perform the ceremony, he was assigned to do the job.

The Smiley staff had less than a day's notice before John was buried. Four staff members were there. It was a very short ceremony, maybe five minutes long. Since the day was bitterly cold and windy, no one was in the mood to linger.

Chairs for the mourners had been placed by the open grave. No one sat in them. Wayne Jordan spoke in a halting way about "ashes to ashes." Mary Wilkerson read an inspirational verse. The funeral service was over. A few flowers were put on John's casket, and everyone left. A few hours later, John was lowered into the ground.

Fate had played one last, bitter card in the life and death of John Doe No. 24. The man who spent his life an obscure, unknown person was buried in an unmarked grave.

Dave Bakke started his newspaper career at a Minnesota weekly in 1975. He began his daily newspaper career in 1978 as a reporter and columnist for the *Journal* in Sioux City, Iowa. In 1983, he became a feature writer and columnist with *The State Journal-Register* in Springfield, Illinois. In 1990, he was named coordinator of that newspaper's Heartland feature magazine. During his career, he has been the recipient of numerous Associated Press and Copley Newspaper awards. In 1992, Bakke won the Penney-Missouri Lifestyle Award sponsored by the University of Missouri School of Journalism. He was the only first-place winner from a paper with a circulation under 250,000. His first book (coauthored with Dale Hamm), *The Last of the Market Hunters,* was published in 1996 by Southern Illinois University Press.